The Temporary Society

Warren Bennis
Philip Slater

The Temporary Society

Jossey-Bass Publishers
San Francisco

Jossey-Bass books and products are available through most bookstores. To contact
Jossey-Bass directly, call (888) 378-2537, fax to (800) 605-2665, or visit our website
at www.josseybass.com.

Substantial discounts on bulk quantities of Jossey-Bass books are available to corporations, professional associations, and other organizations. For details and discount
information, contact the special sales department at Jossey-Bass.

For sales outside the United States, please contact your local Simon & Schuster
International Office.

 Manufactured in the United States of America on Lyons Falls Turin Book.
This paper is acid-free and 100 percent totally chlorine-free.

Library of Congress Cataloging-in-Publication Data

Bennis, Warren G.
 The temporary society / Warren G. Bennis, Philip E. Slater. —
  Rev. ed.
   p. cm. — (The Jossey-Bass business & management series)
  Includes index.
  ISBN 0-7879-4331-2
  1. United States—Social conditions—1945– I. Slater, Philip
Elliot. II. Title. III. Series.
HN58 .B43 1998
306'.0973—ddc21   98-19731

FIRST EDITION
HB Printing   10 9 8 7 6 5 4 3 2 1

The Jossey-Bass
Business & Management Series

Contents

For Grace Gabe and Susan Helgeson

Preface to the Revised Edition

Prediction is a democratic pastime. In authoritarian societies there is little call for it—life is static, change is slow, innovation is tightly controlled, and, on the rare occasions when it occurs, change is announced from above. The wild guesses about the future so popular in our society are meaningless when "the future"—what little there is of it—is funneled through the tiny orifice of centralized authority, which disapproves of attempts to anticipate its leaden decisions.

A democratic society is a complex, confusing, erratic, and continually evolving organism that grows in all directions at once. Making one's way in it calls for an extraordinary degree of alertness, sensitivity, and flexibility. Predictions are made and altered daily as the evolutionary winds shift.

Authoritarians are not happy with this spinning weather vane we take for granted. They want an iron rooster that points every day in exactly the same direction. They don't want predictions; they want predictability. They want to control the uncontrollable, which is why they are so obsessed with disciplining the most spontaneous products of nature: children, animals, and all growing things.

In the past this obsession with control had support from science, with its constant search for "predictability," that is, the certainty that would render "predictions"—guessing the future—unnecessary. But with the advent of the Uncertainty Principle and Chaos Theory, science has now irrevocably committed itself to the democratic camp, to the realization that life, nature, the world around us, all have an agenda and we are a part of it, not the master of it, and must meet it on its own terms.[1] Democracy is not about control. It is about attunement.

Most of us grew up in bureaucratic organizations that were dominated by a command-and-control orientation. This approach was memorialized by the prose of German writer and sociologist Max Weber, who was the first to bring to the world's attention that this bureaucratic machine model is a genius of social invention, designed to harness the manpower and resources of the nineteenth century. Bureaucracies are characterized by strong divisions of labor, narrow specialization, and hierarchies, with lots of levels. Most organizations today still have that kind of command-and-control, macho mentality.

If there are three words that best describe the mind-set of that paradigm, they would be *control, order,* and *predict.* The words yield an interesting acronym: COP.

The organizations of the future will resemble networks or modules. The successful ones will have flattened hierarchies and more cross-functional linkages. The three words that best describe the mind-set of this paradigm are *acknowledge, create,* and *empower.* Those words also yield an interesting acronym: ACE. Given the speed and complexity of change in our society, which affects all management environments, we have no alternative but to move away from COP toward ACE.

The predictions we made in the first edition of this book have come to pass. We said that the Soviet Union would collapse and that by 2018 democracy would encompass the globe. We seem to be well on our way to realizing that state. Most of the authoritarian nations that still exist are backward and poor, as we would expect. Those that are not, like China, are being forced to inch toward democracy, though kicking and screaming all the way. The trend cannot be stopped except by war, for war is the primary reason authoritarianism exists.

For us such predictions seem easy and obvious—much like predicting that spring will follow winter. It might not, of course. An asteroid might hit the earth and knock the seasons out of whack. By the same token, diehard authoritarians might manage to create a global war—always the most feared enemy of democracy. But short of this, the movement toward democracy seems inexorable for all the reasons we have given.

One of the reasons some people have trouble grasping this inevitability is that many of them think of authoritarianism as a "natural" state. After all, it has dominated the planet for the past 6,000 years and permeates our myths, religions, languages, and habits. But for millions of years before that, human beings were hunter-gatherers living in small democratic and egalitarian groups. When we take this larger view, authoritarianism is only a little blip in the lifetime of our species. It arose with the advent of large-scale agriculture and animal husbandry, when the need for large tracts of land and the manpower to work them made slavery economic and organized warfare appealing. But with the emergence of global communication, a global economy, rapid technological change, and planetary consciousness, authoritarianism no longer makes sense. Slavery is uneconomical; war merely destructive; and the old habits, values, social systems, and ways of thinking they gave rise to have become obsolete and counterproductive.

Our prediction was based on the fact that technological change has accelerated to the point that no rigid autocracy can contain it. War—the principal means of accumulating both public and private wealth in preindustrial times—now serves that function for only a few individuals and consistently weakens societies that embrace it. Centralized systems tend to be rigid; they consistently fail to adapt to changing conditions—often shooting the messenger that warns of their approach. They are like the turn-of-the-century tycoon who locked his luckless heirs into streetcar stock "because people will always need transportation." Democracies—despite their sloppy appearance—are more efficient in the face of change because they maximize the impact of those who are not overcommitted to the status quo.

We can predict the spread of democracy but not the direction in which it will lead us. If you think you know where a democracy is heading, you have a fundamental misunderstanding of the form. Democracy continually reinvents itself; it is a process, not a product. Authoritarian systems always have a set goal, a fixed end point, a utopia to be realized, a depot at the end of the track. But democracy is experimental; it proceeds by trial and error. For after all, it is only through errors that we learn, and democracy, if nothing else, is an education.

What follows is essentially unchanged from the original work, except that we have made some of the language more current and added updates at the beginning of each chapter; these reflect our thoughts and reactions to the events of the last three decades. As in the original work, Chapters Two and Four are by Slater; Chapters Three, Five, and Six are by Bennis; the first chapter, like this preface, is a joint effort.

May 1998   WARREN BENNIS
                                              Santa Monica, California

                                                   PHILIP SLATER
                                                Santa Cruz, California

Preface to the Original Edition

Prediction is a risky, difficult, and unrewarding activity in any time, and forecasting social trends even more so. To engage in such an endeavor in a world of unprecedented complexity during changes of unparalleled rapidity is as absurd as it is necessary.

This book is an attempt to relate a few dimensions of modern society—democratic systems of social organization, chronic change, socialization, and interpersonal behavior—to place them in some temporal perspective and to try to envision future combinations. The theses advanced are both exploratory and circumscribed. We have not tried to put forward a grand overarching and inclusive model, like [Marshall] McLuhan, nor have we tried to analyze exhaustively the vicissitudes of one or two manageable variables. We have tried simply to stretch the boundaries of our knowledge by forcing our available resources into domains of the greatest ambiguity.

The history of our collaboration is reflected in the book itself, but its roots go back somewhat earlier. Bennis's ideas about industrial organization and democratic leadership were developed in the late 1950s. Slater's ideas on the relation between democracy, change, and family patterns stemmed from research on role differentiation and on attitudes toward the aged. These parallel strands were combined in our first collaboration, "Democracy Is Inevitable," which, in revised form, appears here as Chapter One.

The attention attracted by this paper and its frequent reprinting encouraged us to extend further the approach attempted there. Each of us delves more deeply in the following chapters into those areas of the original article that he knows most thoroughly. Chapter Two deals with the impact of change and democratization on the American family, and Chapter Three traces this impact on human organization. Having come together and been informed by the collaboration, we each returned to our initial interest and pursued it more or less independently.

In the last two chapters, we intersect once more. Slater carries forward the ideas first advanced on the family in Chapter Two and widens its relevance to the styles of relationships that will become more dominant—nonpermanent relationships. In Chapter Five, Bennis attempts to outline the agenda for leaders and managers of the new-style organizations (adaptive organizations) and to indicate how these new men of power can reach their goals.

We write this book with one main goal, and that is to force into view certain changes affecting vital aspects of our key institutions: organizational life, family life, interpersonal relationships, and authority. The theme that is common to this interweaving is a serious concern with the nature and future of our society and a desire to free ourselves from the restraints of traditional preconceptions and stereotypes about social institutions. Without this perspective, however distorted, we have no chance at all to will and shape our future; we can only back into it.

February 1968

WARREN BENNIS
Buffalo, New York

PHILIP SLATER
Boston, Massachusetts

The Authors

WARREN BENNIS is University Professor and Distinguished Professor of Business Administration and founding chairman of the Leadership Institute of the University of Southern California. He has written twenty-five books, including the best-selling *Leaders* and *On Becoming a Leader*; both have been translated into nineteen languages. The *Financial Times* recently named *Leaders* as one of the top fifty business books of all time. In 1993 Addison-Wesley published a book of his essays, *An Invented Life: Reflections on Leadership and Change*, and Jossey-Bass republished his path-breaking book *Beyond Bureaucracy*. Over one million copies of his books are in print.

He has served on the faculty of MIT's Sloan School of Management, where he was Chairman of the Organizational Studies Department. He is a former faculty member of Harvard University and Boston University, former provost and executive vice president of State University of New York at Buffalo, and former president of the University of Cincinnati. He is a recipient of eleven honorary degrees and serves on the boards of Claremont University Center and the Salk Institute. The *Wall Street Journal* named him as one of the top ten speakers on management, and in 1996 *Forbes* magazine referred to him as the "Dean of Leadership Gurus." His latest book is *Organizing Genius: The Secrets of Creative Collaboration*, published in 1997 by Addison-Wesley.

PHILIP SLATER was professor and chairperson of the Department of Sociology at Brandeis University until he left in 1971 to become a freelance writer. He is the author of nine books of nonfiction, including *The Glory of Hera, A Dream Deferred,* and the best-seller *The Pursuit of Loneliness.* Although his novel *How I Saved the World* was voted one of the ten best books of 1985 by the San Diego Union, he remains loyal to Northern California.

The Temporary Society

1

Democracy Is Inevitable[1]

———◆◆◆———

Today the inevitability of democracy might seem obvious, but in the mid–sixties, when we first argued that democracy would eventually dominate in both the world and the workplace, a nuclear war between the United States and the Soviet Union seemed more likely than a McDonald's in Moscow.

It all started because Bennis had seen a common thread running through the most exciting organizations of that time: as the once absolute power of top management atrophied, a more collegial organization was emerging where good ideas were valued—even if they weren't the boss's ideas. We became convinced that democracy would triumph for a simple but utterly compelling reason: it was working. It was, and is, more effective than autocracy, bureaucracy, or any other nondemocratic form of organization. We went on later to develop these ideas more fully: Bennis through his extensive work on leadership and organization,[2] and Slater in an exploration of democracy's cultural and psychological underpinnings.[3]

In international politics democratization is a very recent phenomenon, albeit a profound one. A decade ago Nicolae Ceausescu had the power to ban birth control in Romania and require that every typewriter be registered. The state even regulated the temperature of Romanian households. The collapse of his regime was even more remarkable for being so long in coming.

The democratization of the workplace has made fewer headlines but has been no less dramatic. In the sixties participative management was considered so radical that some of the Sloan Fellows at the Massachusetts Institute of Technology accused Bennis of being a communist for espousing it. Today most major corporations practice some form of egalitarian management. The pyramid-shaped organization chart is going the way of the Edsel.

The change is pervasive. Self-managed work groups are replacing assembly lines in auto plants. Organizations as disparate as Herman Miller (the manufacturer of office furniture) and Beth Israel in Boston have adopted the democratic management techniques of the late Joseph Scanlon—one of the first to appreciate that employee involvement is crucial for quality control. At Hewlett-Packard's facility in Greeley, Colorado, most decisions are made not by traditional managers but by frontline employees who work in teams on parts of projects. Even project coordination is done by team representatives, working on committees known as "boards of directors."

No longer a monolith, the successful modern corporation is like a Lego set whose parts can be regularly reconfigured as circumstances change. The old paradigm that exalted control, order, and predictability is giving way to a nonhierarchical order in which all employees' contributions are solicited and acknowledged and in which creativity is valued over blind loyalty. Sheer self-interest motivates the change. Organizations that encourage broad participation, even dissent, make better decisions. Rebecca A. Henry, a psychology professor at Purdue University, found that groups are better forecasters than individuals are.[4] And the more the group disagrees initially, the more accurate the forecast is likely to be.

We said that adaptability would become the most important determinant of an organization's survival and that information would drive the organization of the future. This seems even more true today. The person who has information wields more power than ever before. But although we sensed how important processing technology would be, we didn't fully appreciate the extent to which the new technology would accelerate the pace of change and help create a global corporation if not a global village. New York Life Insurance, for example, processes its claims not in New York or even the United States but in Ireland. And a decade ago, when Bennis invited the Dalai Lama to participate in a seminar for CEOs at the University of Southern California, the embodiment of thousands of years of Tibetan spiritualism graciously declined by fax.

Our crystal ball let us down in a few other areas. We failed, for example, to foresee the extraordinary role Japan would play in shaping U.S. corporate behavior in the 1980s. The discovery that another nation could challenge U.S. dominance in the marketplace inspired massive self-evaluation and forever disrupted the status quo. Nothing contributed more to the democratization of business than the belief—true or false—that Japanese management was more consensual than U.S. management. To meet Japanese competition, U.S. leaders were willing to try anything—even share their traditional prerogatives with subordinates.

More surprising is our failure to anticipate the women's movement—a failure reflected in the gender-biased language scattered throughout the original book. For while the women's movement was only embryonic in the sixties, we of all people might have been expected to comment on it since nothing could have been a stronger validation of the points we were making. We said that those who are not overcommitted to the status quo are in the best position to take advantage of change and innovation, and this certainly applies to women, who have pretty much been excluded from the authoritarian hierarchical structures that have dominated human existence for the past 6,000 years. As men were squeezed by authoritarian culture into the emotional corset of macho competitiveness, it fell to women to take care of all other human needs—emotional expression, relationships, cooperation, nurturance, and so on. They were forced to become skilled at diplomacy, mediation, negotiation, compromise, recognition of the needs and rights of others, and so on. But these are precisely the skills that are needed in a democracy. Men who practice democracy tend still to be caught up in the belligerent assumptions of the authoritarian past: they talk constantly of "standing up to" and "not being swayed by" and "not giving in to" and being "firm" or "tough," as if rigidity were a virtue and problem solving a form of hand-to-hand combat.

Men have committed themselves to an individualistic, linear, competitive, atomistic, and mechanistic conceptual world—one which they now dominate. But ironically, science—once the most extreme expression of this world—has now rendered it obsolete. Recent advances in physics and biology have opened up an entirely new conceptual universe.[5] The cosmos, scientists have begun to realize, is not a mechanism constructed of little particles that can be taken apart and put together—it is a gigantic unity of which the significant elements are *relationships*.

In the past men disparaged this way of looking at the world as "magical thinking," typical of women, children, and the inhabitants of nonliterate societies. But now it has become the accepted conceptual framework as we enter the next century. Nature, it seems, is relentlessly nonlinear, and those who fail to recognize this simple truth are destined to be left behind, mired in an antiquated mind-set.

Women are better adapted to the confusion and chaos that chronic change, democracy, and the new sciences together produce. Their control needs, on average, tend to be less exaggerated than those of men, who like to dominate their environment and make it simple and predictable. Women are more comfortable with the chaos that small children generate and are better able to cope with several different processes at the same time. The traditional housewife trying to cook, clean, and shop while noisy children were racing everywhere received optimum training for democratic living.

Some will object, of course, that women who become corporate managers do not necessarily exhibit these traits but are often more controlling, rigid, competitive, and authoritarian than men. This will be true as long as women are a small minority in a "man's world," having to prove they have traits they are not expected to have—having to show they are "tough" enough to do the job. In the same way, blacks who have succeeded in the same situation have often had to be "whiter" than whites—more conservative, uptight, restrained, and so forth. Once a group ceases to be a rarity, this need to over-conform to tradition eases.

In the first edition we predicted that industrial nations would eventually be forced to democratize, and this prediction has been borne out. Democracy movements in satellite states such as Poland and Czechoslovakia, as well as in capitalist countries like South Korea and South Africa, continue to demonstrate the long-range incompatibility of modern technological innovation and authoritarianism.

We also predicted that dictatorships would characterize developing nations in their early stages, and this, too, has been borne out. While the more viable states of Latin America and Asia are being pushed toward democracy, most third-world countries still find themselves mired in autocratic regimes. Yet even in Africa—plagued in recent decades by war, famine, and poverty—signs of change have been observed: "After decades of trying to impose centralized systems, governments [are beginning to] allow businessmen and villagers to take the lead . . . Democracy has softened dictatorial rule in a score of countries. Although flawed and often fixed, elections allow harsh criticism of leaders who once stifled any hint of dissent." And in a rare reversal of the macho ethic that has helped keep so much of Africa enslaved and impoverished for so long, Senegalese President Abdou Diouf observed that "women are the key" to this development.[6]

In recent years our understanding of democracy has been enhanced by new data on early civilizations, particularly the work of Riane Eisler.[7] Drawing on a wealth of archeological data,[8] Eisler effectively demolishes the popular assumption that authoritarianism and war are somehow "natural" to human beings. She demonstrates that the "Golden Age" so often mentioned by the Greeks refers to an actual period of peace and equality in Europe and the Mediterranean, with a much higher level of culture than previously believed. In Minoan Crete, for example, there were no kings or nobles, and war was almost unknown until Crete's last days. Yet a level of civilization had been achieved that was not equaled for more than a millennium.

Eisler also lays to rest the notion that authoritarianism and belligerence are somehow part of our primate heritage, pointing to the Bonobos—a species closely related to the chimpanzee, but one in which dominating behavior is absent, conflicts are resolved through sexual seduction, and the least aggressive males are those chosen by the females as partners.[9] Slater elaborates the relationship between democracy and the women's movement in A Dream Deferred.[10]

The growth of democratic systems in industry has accelerated since the first edition. In a survey of 1,000 corporations Lawler[11] found that 80 percent used some form of participatory management. And as we noted then, it is particularly common in companies engaged in invention, such as electronics. Companies on the cutting edge of technological change tend to be forced by their very nature to operate by democratic principles, and those that become bureaucratized and hierarchical usually find themselves quickly upstaged by egalitarian newcomers. Adams and Brock[12] point out that "very small firms produce twenty-four times as many innovations per research and development dollar as large corporations," and although size is not inherently related to authoritarianism, the correlation is historically a large one.

One of the concerns of 1968 that we refer to seems rather quaint today. This was the fear that the trend toward more democratic structures in the corporate world would lead to a nation of homogeneous "Organization Men"—colorless and interchangeable ciphers, willingly serving an impersonal corporate machine. The key word here is *willingly*. Although a great many workers and managers today may feel themselves caught in such a predicament—as they have for the last century or more—the notion that they will somehow have been brainwashed into accepting it seems dated. And homogeneity, which once held a proud position in the top ten of our national fears, right after the Red Menace, has become, in the age of multiculturalism and our obsession with "lifestyles," merely the fond dream of a few bigoted white males.

Transitions are difficult. The gradual global shift from authoritarianism to democracy—from war to peace, from machismo to cooperation, from domination to attunement, from linear science to nonlinear science—is a paradigm shift of unprecedented magnitude. Such a change inevitably causes great strain and confusion for us poor human beings hungry for stability and familiarity. We reach excitedly toward the future with one hand and cling desperately to our old concepts with the other. Is it any wonder we feel pulled apart at times? We can see this strain in the so-called lack of civility in our daily lives today, in the frustration that produces so much ranting on the airwaves and so often leads to violence. We see our ambivalence in our high-tech sci-fi fantasies that begin with so much sophistication but usually end in some form of hand-to-hand combat. We see it again in our many movies about brutal post-apocalyptic worlds—worlds created by the disastrous macho values we now embrace, yet at the same time rendering those same values once again meaningful and desirable.

Reality is less dramatic. Change is a gradual, two-steps-forward-one-back process, but we may reasonably be expected to muddle through. There will be plenty of disasters and atrocities along the way for change never comes cheaply. Nobody likes becoming obsolete, and those who hold advantages seldom give them up without a struggle. But the process cannot be stopped without a global catastrophe; it gathers momentum every day. It will never be easy for us, but it may help a little to recognize what's happening and to admit that it all makes us a little uncomfortable, whether we think we welcome change or fight it tooth and nail.

We argued in the first edition that the military-bureaucratic model was becoming increasingly obsolete and being replaced by a scientific one. This is still true. Science not only tolerates change, it creates change. And as we wrote, science flourishes only in a democracy—the one form of organization recognizing that creativity is invaluable, unpredictable, and can come from any quarter.

———————

Cynical observers have always been fond of pointing out that business leaders who extol the virtues of democracy on ceremonial occasions would be the last to think of applying them to their own organizations. To the extent that this is true, however, it reflects a state of mind that by no means is peculiar to businessmen but that characterizes all Americans—perhaps all citizens of democracies.

This attitude, briefly, is that democracy is a nice way of life for nice people, despite its manifold inconveniences—a kind of expensive and inefficient luxury, like owning a large medieval castle. Feelings about it are for the most part affectionate, even respectful, but a little impatient. There are probably few men of affairs in America who have not at some time nourished in their hearts the blasphemous thought that life would go much more smoothly if democracy could be relegated to some kind of Sunday morning devotion.

The bluff practicality of the "nice-but-inefficient" stereotype masks a hidden idealism, however, for it implies that institutions can survive in a competitive environment through the sheer goodheartedness of those who maintain them. We would like to challenge this notion and suggest that even if all of those benign sentiments were eradicated today, we would awaken tomorrow to find democracy still firmly entrenched, buttressed by a set of economic, social, and political forces as practical as they are uncontrollable.

We will argue that democracy has been so widely embraced, not because of some vague yearning for human rights but because *under certain conditions* it is a more "efficient" form of social organization. We do not regard it as accidental that those nations of the world that have endured longest under conditions of relative wealth and stability are democratic, whereas authoritarian regimes have, with few exceptions, either crumbled or maintained a precarious and backward existence.

Despite this evidence, even so acute a statesman as Adlai Stevenson argued in a *New York Times* article on November 4, 1962, that the goals of the Communists are different from ours. "They are interested in power," he said, "we in community. With such fundamentally different aims, how is it possible to compare communism and democracy in terms of efficiency? You might as well ask whether a locomotive is more efficient than a symphony orchestra."

Isn't this simply the speech of an articulate man who believes that democracy is inefficient and doesn't like to say so? Actually we are concerned with locomotives *and* symphony orchestras, with power *and* community. The challenges for communism and democracy are, in fact, identical: to compete successfully for the world's resources and imagination.

Our position is, in brief, that democracy (whether capitalistic or socialistic is not at issue here) is the only system that can successfully cope with the changing demands of contemporary civilization.

We are not necessarily endorsing democracy as such; one might reasonably argue that industrial civilization is pernicious and should be abolished. We suggest merely that given a desire to survive in this civilization, democracy is the most effective means to achieve this end.

There are signs, in fact, that our business community is becoming aware of this law. Several of the newest and most rapidly blooming companies in the United States boast unusually democratic organizations. Even more surprising is the fact that some of the largest of the established corporations have been moving steadily, if accidentally, toward democratization. Frequently they began by feeling that administrative vitality and creativity were lacking in the older systems of organization. In increasing numbers, therefore, they enlisted the support of social scientists and of outside programs, the net effect of which has been to democratize their organization. Executives and even entire management staffs have been sent to participate in human relations and organizational laboratories to learn skills and attitudes that ten years ago would have been denounced as anarchic and revolutionary. At these meetings, status prerogatives and traditional concepts of authority are severely challenged.

Many social scientists have played an important role in this development toward humanizing and democratizing large-scale bureaucracies. The theories of McGregor, Likert, Argyris, and Blake paved the way to a new social architecture. Research and training centers at the National Training Laboratories, Tavistock Institute, Massachusetts Institute of Technology, Harvard Business School, Boston University, University of California at Los Angeles, Case Institute of Technology, and others have pioneered in the application of social-scientific knowledge to the improvement of organizational effectiveness. So far, the data are not all in; conclusive evidence is missing, but the forecast seems to hold genuine promise: it is possible to bring about greater organizational effectiveness through the utilization of valid social knowledge.[13]

What we have in mind when we use the term *democracy* is not *permissiveness* or *laissez-faire* but a system of values—a climate of beliefs governing behavior—that people are internally compelled to affirm by deeds as well as words. These values include

1. Full and free *communication*, regardless of rank and power
2. A reliance on *consensus*, rather than the more customary forms of coercion or compromise to manage conflict
3. The idea that *influence* is based on technical competence and knowledge rather than on the vagaries of personal whims or prerogatives of power
4. An atmosphere that permits and even encourages emotional expression as well as task-oriented acts
5. A basically human bias, one that accepts the inevitability of conflict between the organization and the individual but that is willing to cope with and mediate this conflict on rational grounds

Changes along these dimensions are being promoted widely in American industry. Most important, for our analysis, is what we believe to be the reason for these changes: *democracy becomes a functional necessity whenever a social system is competing for survival under conditions of chronic change.*

The most familiar variety of such change to the inhabitants of the modern world is technological innovation. Because change has now become a permanent and accelerating factor in American life, adaptability to change becomes increasingly the most important single determinant of survival. The profit, the saving, the efficiency, the morale of the moment becomes secondary to keeping the door open for rapid readjustment to changing conditions.

Organization and communication research at the Massachusetts Institute of Technology reveals quite dramatically what type of organization is best suited for which kind of environment. Specifically:

for simple tasks under static conditions, an autocratic, centralized structure such as has characterized most industrial organizations in the past, is quicker, neater, and more efficient. But for adaptability to changing conditions, for rapid acceptance of a new idea, for "flexibility in dealing with novel problems, generally high morale and loyalty the more egalitarian or decentralized type seems to work better." One of the reasons for this is that the centralized decision maker is "apt to discard an idea on the grounds that he is too busy or the idea too impractical."[14] The failure of Nazi Germany to develop the atom bomb is a telling example of this phenomenon.

Our argument for democracy rests on an additional factor, one that is fairly complicated but profoundly important in shaping our ideas. First of all, it is interesting to note that modern industrial organization has been based roughly on the antiquated system of the military. Relics of the military system of thought can still be found in terminology such as "line and staff," "standard operating procedure," "table of organization," and so on. Other remnants can be seen in the emotional and mental assumptions regarding work and motivation held today by some managers and industrial consultants.

By and large these conceptions are changing, and even the military is moving away from the oversimplified and questionable assumptions on which its organization was originally based. The Israeli army, for example, is unsurpassed throughout the world for sheer military effectiveness. It is also one of the most slovenly, equalitarian, and democratic. Spit and polish is ignored; social barriers between officers and men are almost nonexistent; and communication of ideas proceeds up as well as down the rank hierarchy. Even more striking, as we have mentioned, are developments taking place in industry. These are no less profound than a fundamental change away from the autocratic and arbitrary vagaries of the past toward democratic decision making.

This change has been coming about because of the palpable inadequacy of the military-bureaucratic model, particularly its response to rapid change, and also because the institution of science is now emerging as a more suitable model.[15]

But why is science gaining acceptance as a model? Most certainly, it is *not* because we teach and conduct research within research-oriented universities. Curiously enough, universities have been stubbornly resistant to democratization, far more so than most other institutions.

We believe that science is winning out because the challenges facing modern enterprises are, at base, knowledge-gathering, truth-requiring dilemmas. Managers are not scientists, nor do we expect them to be. But the processes of solving problems, resolving conflicts, and recognizing dilemmas have great kinship with the academic pursuit of truth. The institution of science is the only institution based on and geared for change. It is built not only to adapt to change but to overthrow and create change. So it is—and will be—with modern industrial enterprises.

And here we come to the point. In order for the spirit of inquiry—the foundation of science—to grow and flourish, a democratic environment is a necessity. Science encourages a political view that is egalitarian, pluralistic, liberal. It accentuates freedom of opinion and dissent. It is against all forms of totalitarianism, dogma, mechanization, and blind obedience. As a prominent social psychologist has pointed out, "Men have asked for freedom, justice and respect precisely as science has spread among them."[16] In short, we believe that the only way in which organizations can ensure a scientific *attitude* is by providing conditions where it can flourish. Very simply, this means democratic social conditions.

In other words, democracy in industry is not an idealistic conception but a hard necessity in those areas in which change is ever-present and in which creative scientific enterprise must be nourished. For democracy is the only system of organization that is compatible with perpetual change.

It might be objected here that we have been living in an era of rapid technological change for a hundred years without any noticeable change in the nature of the average industrial firm. True, there are now many restrictions on the power of the executive over his subordinates compared with those prevailing at the end of the nineteenth century. But this hardly constitutes industrial democracy; the decision-making function is still an exclusive and jealously guarded prerogative of the top echelons. If democracy is an inevitable consequence of perpetual change, why then have we not seen more dramatic changes in the structure of industrial organizations? The answer is twofold.

First, the rate of technological change is rapidly accelerating. Take advance in scientific knowledge as one criterion: it doubles every ten years. Casamir calculated that if the *Physical Review* continued to grow as rapidly as it had between 1945 and 1960, it would weigh more than the earth during the next century.[17] Prior to World War I a businessman might live a productive and successful life and find himself outmoded at the end of it. By the end of World War II a similar man could find that his training, skills, outlook, and ways of thinking were obsolescent in the middle of his career. James R. Killian, Jr., chairman of the Corporation of Massachusetts Institute of Technology, estimated that already [in 1963] several hundred thousand engineers are obsolete.[18] This is undoubtedly matched by an equal number of managers.

We are now beginning an era when a man's knowledge and approach can become obsolete before he has even begun the career for which he was trained. The value of what one learns is always slipping away, like the value of money in runaway inflation. We are living in an era that could be characterized as a runaway inflation of knowledge and skill, and it is this that is, perhaps, responsible for the feelings of futility, alienation, and lack of individual worth that are said to characterize our time.

Under such conditions, the individual is of relatively little significance. No matter how imaginative, energetic, and brilliant he may be, time will soon catch up with him to the point where he can profitably be replaced by someone equally imaginative, energetic, and brilliant but with a more up-to-date viewpoint and fewer obsolete preconceptions. As Martin Gardner says, with regard to the difficulty some physicists have in grasping Einstein's theory of relativity, "If you are young, you have a great advantage over these scientists. Your mind has not yet developed those deep furrows along which thoughts so often are forced to travel."[19] This situation is just beginning to be felt as an immediate reality in American industry, and it is this kind of uncontrollably rapid change that generates democratization.

The second reason is that the mere existence of a dysfunctional tendency, such as the relatively slow adaptability of authoritarian structures, does not automatically bring about its disappearance. This drawback must either first be recognized for what it is or become so severe as to destroy the structures in which it is embedded. Both of these conditions are only now beginning to make themselves felt, primarily through the peculiar nature of modern technological competition.

The crucial change has been that the threat of technological defeat no longer comes necessarily from rivals within the industry, who usually can be imitated quickly without too great a loss, but often from outside—from new industries using new materials in new ways. One can therefore make no intelligent prediction about "what the next likely development in our industry will be." The blow may come from anywhere. Correspondingly, a viable corporation cannot merely develop and advance in the usual ways. In order to survive and grow it must be prepared to go anywhere—to develop new products or techniques even if they are irrelevant to the present activities of the organization.[20] It is perhaps for this reason that the beginnings of democratization have appeared most often in industries (such as electronics) that depend heavily on invention. Marshall McLuhan [influential social scientist of the 1960s and 1970s] no doubt exaggerated when he said that "no new idea ever starts from within a big operation. It must assail the organization from outside, through some small but competing organization."[21]

But it helps explain why more and more sprawling behemoths are planning consequential changes in their organizational structures and climates toward releasing democratic potentiality.

This issue is frequently misunderstood. People argue that Nazi Germany was an exception to our rule, because it was at once highly authoritarian and highly efficient. But the fact that the organization destroyed itself in foolish military adventures is excluded from the criterion of efficiency in this example, as if survival were a detail of no importance. This is a common fallacy in industry: a management that saves a hundred thousand dollars through cost-cutting measures and provokes, in the process, a million-dollar wildcat strike, is more likely to be called efficient than one that saves $900,000 by doing neither! Men strive for efficiency within a narrowly defined range of familiar acts and relegate all other events to the category of "acts of God," as if no one could expect to exert any control over them. The martinet general whose beautifully disciplined fighting machine is wiped out by guerrillas will probably still lay claim to efficiency, but we need not agree with his assumption that efficiency consists in doing an irrelevant thing well. By such a definition the March Hare was efficient when he used the "best butter" to repair the Mad Hatter's watch. The Greeks cautioned against calling a man happy before he had achieved a peaceful death; we would caution against calling any organization efficient until it has met at least one new and unexpected threat to its existence.

The passing of years has also given the *coup de grâce* to another force that retarded democratization—the Great Man who with brilliance and farsightedness could preside with dictatorial powers at the head of a growing organization and keep it at the vanguard of American business. In the past he was usually a man with a single idea, or a constellation of related ideas, which he developed brilliantly. This is no longer enough (and the Great Man may, in fact, be a Great Woman).

Today, just as the head of an organization begins to reap the harvest of his imagination, he finds that someone else (even, perhaps, one of his stodgier competitors, aroused by desperation) has suddenly carried the innovation a step further, or has found an entirely new and superior approach to it, and he is suddenly outmoded. How easily can he abandon his idea, which contains all his hopes, his ambitions, his very heart? His aggressiveness now begins to turn in on his own organization, and the absolutism of his position begins to be a liability, a dead hand, an iron shackle upon the flexibility and growth of the company. But he cannot be removed. In the short run the firm would even be hurt by his loss, since its prestige derives to such an extent from his reputation. And by the time he has left, the organization will have receded into a secondary position within the industry. It may even decay further when his personal touch is lost.

The cult of personality still exists, of course, but it is rapidly fading. More and more large corporations predicate their growth not on heroes but on solid management teams.

Taking the place of the Great Man, we are often told, is the organization man. A good many tears have been shed over this transition by liberals and conservatives alike. The liberals, of course, have in mind, as the individual, some sort of creative deviant—an intellectual, artist, or radical politician. The conservatives are thinking of the old captains of industry and perhaps some great generals.

Neither is at all unhappy to lose the individuals mourned by the other, dismissing them contemptuously as Communists and rabble-rousers, on the one hand, and criminals and Fascists, on the other. What is particularly confusing in terms of the present issue is a tendency to equate conformity with autocracy, to see the new industrial organization as one in which all individualism is lost except for a few villainous individualistic manipulators at the top.

But this, of course, is absurd in the long run. The trend toward the organization man is also a trend toward a looser and more flexible organization in which roles are to some extent interchangeable and no one is indispensable. To many people this trend is a monstrous nightmare, but one should at least not confuse it with the nightmares of the past. It may mean anonymity and homogeneity, but it does not and cannot mean authoritarianism, in the long run, despite the bizarre anomalies and hybrids that may arise in a period of transition.

The reason it cannot is that it arises out of a need for flexibility and adaptability. Democracy and the dubious trend toward the organization man (for this trend *is* a part of democratization, whether we like this aspect of democracy or not) both arise from the need to maximize the availability of appropriate knowledge, skill, and insight under conditions of great variability.

While the organization man idea has titillated the imagination of the American public, it has masked a far more fundamental change now taking place: the rise of the "professional man." Professional specialists, holding advanced degrees in such abstruse sciences as cryogenics or computer logic, as well as the more mundane business disciplines, are entering all types of organizations at a higher rate than any other sector of the labor market.

And these men can hardly be called organization men. They seemingly derive their rewards from inward standards of excellence, from their professional societies, from the intrinsic satisfaction of their standards, and not from their bosses. Because they have degrees, they travel. They are not good company men; they are uncommitted except to the challenging environments where they can "play with problems."

These new professional men are remarkably compatible with our conception of a democratic system. For, like these new men, democracy seeks no new stability, no end point; it is purposeless, save that it purports to ensure perpetual transition, constant alteration, ceaseless instability. It attempts to upset nothing but only to facilitate the potential upset of anything. Democracy and our new professional men identify primarily with the adaptive process, not the establishment.

Yet it must also be remembered that all democratic systems are not entirely so—there are always limits to the degree of fluidity that can be borne. Thus, it is not a contradiction to the theory of democracy to find that a particular democratic society or organization may be more conservative than some autocratic one. Indeed, the most dramatic violent and drastic changes have always taken place under autocratic regimes, for such changes usually require prolonged self-denial, while democracy rarely lends itself to such voluntary asceticism. But these changes have been viewed as finite and temporary, aimed at a specific set of reforms, and moving toward a new state of nonchange. It is only when the society reaches a level of technological development in which survival is dependent on the institutionalization of perpetual change that democracy becomes necessary.

The [former] Soviet Union experienced this change; the United States has also. Yet democratic institutions existed in the United States when it was still an agrarian nation. Indeed, democracy has existed in many places and at many times, long before the advent of modern technology. How can we account for these facts?

In the first place, it must be remembered that modern technology is not the only factor that could give rise to conditions of necessary perpetual change. Any situation involving rapid and unplanned expansion, sustained over a sufficient period of time, will tend to produce great pressure for democratization. Second, when we speak of democracy we are referring not only, or even primarily, to a particular political format. Indeed, American egalitarianism has perhaps its most important manifestation, not in the constitution, but in the family.

Historians are fond of pointing out that Americans have always lived under expanding conditions—first the frontier, then the successive waves of immigration, now a runaway technology. The social effects of these kinds of expansions are, of course, profoundly different in many ways, but they share one impact in common: all have made it impossible for an authoritarian family system to develop on a large scale. Every foreign observer of American mores since the seventeenth century has commented that American children have no respect for their parents, and every generation of

Americans since 1650 has produced forgetful native moralists complaining about the decline in filial obedience and deference (see Chapter Two).

It was not so much American ways that shook up the old family patterns but the demands and requirements of a new situation. How could the young look to the old as the ultimate fount of wisdom and knowledge when, in fact, the old knowledge was irrelevant—when, indeed, the children had a better practical grasp of the realities of American life than did their elders? How many of the latter can keep up with their children in knowledge of the sciences, for example? Santayana put it beautifully when he said: "No specific hope about distant issues is ever likely to be realized. The ground shifts, the will of mankind deviates, and what the father dreamt of the children neither fulfill nor desire."[22]

It is this fact that reveals the basis for the association between democracy and change. The old, the learned, the powerful, the wealthy, those in authority—these are the ones who are committed. They have learned a pattern and have succeeded in it. But when change comes, it is often the *uncommitted* who can best realize it, take advantage of it.

Democracy is a superior technique for making the uncommitted more available. The price it exacts is the pain of uninvolvement, alienation, and skepticism. The benefits it gives are flexibility and the joy of confronting new dilemmas.

Indeed, we may even in this way account for the poor opinion democracy has of itself. We underrate the strength of democracy because democracy creates a general attitude of doubt, of skepticism, of modesty. It is only among the authoritarian that we find the dogmatic confidence, the self-righteousness, the intolerance and cruelty that permit one never to doubt oneself and one's beliefs. The looseness, the sloppiness, and the untidiness of democratic structures express the feeling that what has been arrived at today is probably only a partial solution and may well have to be changed tomorrow.

In other words, one cannot believe that change is in itself a good thing and still believe implicitly in the rightness of the present. Judging from the report of history, democracy has always underrated itself—one cannot find a democracy anywhere without also discovering (side-by-side with expressions of outrageous chauvinism) an endless pile of contemptuous and exasperated denunciations of it. And perhaps this is only appropriate. For when a democracy ceases finding fault with itself, it has probably ceased to be a democracy.

But feeling doubt about our own social system need not lead us to overestimate the virtues and efficiency of others. We can find this kind of overestimation in the exaggerated fear of the Red Menace, mere exposure to which is seen as leading to automatic conversion. Few authoritarians can conceive of the possibility that an individual could encounter an authoritarian ideology and not be swept away by it.

Of a similar nature, but more widespread, is the "better dead than Red" mode of thinking. Here again we find an underlying assumption that communism is socially, economically, and ideologically inevitable—that once the military struggle is lost, all is lost. It is interesting that in all our gloomy war speculations, there is never any mention of an American underground movement. It is everywhere assumed that if a war had been fought in which anyone survived and the Soviet Union had won, then

All Americans would immediately become Communists.

The Soviet Union would set up an exact replica of herself in this country.

It would work.

The Soviet system would remain unchanged.

The Soviets in America would be uninfluenced by what they found here.

Not only are these assumptions patently ridiculous; they also reveal a profound misconception about the nature of social systems.

The structure of a society is not determined merely by a belief. It cannot be maintained if it does not work, that is, if no one, not even those in power, is benefiting from it. How many times in history have less-civilized nations conquered more-civilized ones only to be entirely transformed by the cultural influence of their victims? Do we then feel ourselves to be less civilized than the Soviet Union? Is our system so brittle and theirs so enduring?

Actually, quite the contrary seems to be the case. For while democracy seems to be on a fairly sturdy basis in the United States (despite the efforts of self-appointed vigilantes to subvert it), there is considerable evidence that autocracy is beginning to decay in the Soviet Union and in Eastern Europe.

Most Americans have great difficulty in evaluating the facts when confronted with evidence in the Soviet Union of decentralization, of relaxation of repressive controls, or of greater tolerance for criticism. We seem bewildered. And we do not seem to sense the contradiction when we say that these changes were made in response to public discontent. For have we not also believed deeply that an authoritarian regime, if efficiently run, can get away with ignoring the public's clamor? Yet it is now evident that "de-Stalinization" took place because the rigid, repressive authoritarianism of the Stalin era was inefficient, and that many additional relaxations have been forced on the Soviet Union by the necessity of remaining amenable to technological innovation.

But the inevitable Soviet drift toward a more democratic structure is not dependent on the realism of leaders. Leaders come from communities and families, and their patterns of thought are shaped by their experiences with authority in early life, as well as by their sense of what the traffic will bear. We saw that the roots of American democracy were to be found in the nature of the American family. What does the Russian family tell us in this respect?

Pessimism regarding the ultimate destiny of Soviet political life has always been based on the seemingly endless capacity of the Russian people for submission to authoritarian rule. Their tolerance for autocratic rulers was only matched by their autocratic family system, which was equal to the German, the Chinese, or that of many Latin countries in its demand for filial obedience. On this early experience in the family the acceptance of authoritarian rule was based.

But modern revolutionary movements, both fascist and communist, have tended to regard the family with some suspicion as the preserver of old ways and as a possible refuge from the state. Fascist dictators have extolled its conservatism but have tended at times to set up competitive loyalties for the young. Communist revolutionaries, on the other hand, have more unambivalently attacked family loyalty as reactionary, and have deliberately undermined familial allegiances, partly to increase loyalty to the state and partly to facilitate industrialization and modernization by discrediting traditional mores.

Such destruction of authoritarian family patterns is a two-edged sword, which eventually cuts away political autocracy as well as the familial variety. The state may attempt to train submission in its own youth organizations, but so long as the family remains as an institution, this earlier and more enduring experience will outweigh all others. And if the family has been forced by the state to be less authoritarian, the result is obvious.

In creating a youth that has a knowledge, a familiarity, and a set of attitudes more appropriate for successful living in the changing culture than those of its parents, the autocratic state has created a Frankenstein monster that will eventually sweep away the authoritarianism in which it is founded. Russian attempts during the late 1930s to reverse their stand on the family perhaps reflect some realization of this fact. More recent denunciations of Soviet artists and intellectuals also reflect fear of a process going beyond what was originally intended (see Chapter Two).

Further, what the derogation of parental wisdom and authority has begun, the fierce drive for technological modernization will finish. Each generation of youth will be better adapted to the changing society than its parents. And each generation of parents will feel increasingly modest and doubtful about overvaluing its wisdom and superiority as it recognizes the brevity of its usefulness.[23]

We cannot, of course, predict what forms democratization might take in any nation of the world, nor should we become unduly optimistic about its impact on international relations. Although our thesis predicts the ultimate democratization of the entire globe, this is a view so long-range as to be academic. There are infinite opportunities for global extermination before any such stage of development can be achieved.

We should expect that in the earlier stages of industrialization dictatorial regimes will prevail in all of the less-developed nations. We may expect many political grotesques, some of them dangerous in the extreme, to emerge during this long period of transition, as one society after another attempts to crowd the most momentous social changes into a generation or two, working from the most varied structural baselines.

But barring some sudden decline in the rate of technological change, and on the (outrageous) assumption that war will somehow be eliminated during the next half-century, it is possible to predict that after this time democracy will be universal. Each revolutionary autocracy, as it reshuffles the family structure and pushes toward industrialization, will sow the seeds of its own destruction, and democratization will gradually engulf it. Lord Acton once remarked about Christianity that it isn't that people have tried it and found it wanting. It is that they have been afraid to try it and found it impossible. The same comment may have once applied to democracy, but the outlook has changed to the point where people may have to try it.

We may, of course, rue the day. A world of mass democracies may well prove homogenized and ugly. It is perhaps beyond human social capacity to maximize both equality and understanding, on the one hand, and diversity, on the other. Faced with this dilemma, however, many people are willing to sacrifice quaintness to social justice, and just as Marx, in proclaiming the inevitability of communism, did not hesitate to give some assistance to the wheels of fate, so our thesis that democracy represents the social system of the electronic era should not bar these persons from giving a little push here and there to the inevitable.

2

Social Change and
the Democratic Family

Many people feel we are no longer the child-oriented society we once were. They say American adults today are only interested in our personal gratification and advancement, to which we are quite willing to sacrifice our children's future. They cite the federal deficit, the despoiling of the environment, the anticipated collapse of Social Security and Medicare, the precipitous decline in funds for education, the increasing inaccessibility of a college education for all but the very wealthy, the soaring cost of housing, and the evaporation of skilled jobs. They point to the negation of what for centuries has been a national axiom—that most American children can count on having a more affluent lifestyle than their parents.

But while these political changes may possibly reflect some deep-seated ambivalence toward youth—an unconscious wish, played out in the dim regions of public policy, that children suffer and travail as much as their parents did—it does not seem to have affected child-rearing practices to any noticeable degree. Despite all the talk of "tough love" and the value of limits and discipline, the parental norm in the United States is still a child-centered one. There are, of course, constant fulminations against this leniency, as there have been ever since the Pilgrims landed, but the child-centered approach persists unabated.

There has, however, been one significant change in the lives of American children, and while on the surface it seems harmless enough, it may not bode well for the future of American democracy.

It may even have something to do with voter apathy and the view (constantly fanned by the media) that Americans have no interest in "politics," that is, in the decisions that most significantly affect their personal lives. This willingness to leave decision making to others—this tendency to feel that the rules governing the way Americans live and work are out of their control and somehow irrelevant to their immediate interests—may have its roots in the increasing intrusion of adults into the world of children's play.

In the first edition I argued that each generation of Americans has been able to establish its autonomy from its elders through "the insulated life of the age-segregated school and play group" (p. 50).

But how "insulated" is that play group today? Fifty years ago children at play outside of school were self-governing. Playing on makeshift fields, streets, or yards, they had to formulate rules to deal with obstacles, irregular boundaries, odd numbers of players, and the absence of ideal equipment. They were on their own and had to police themselves. This was ideal training for democracy, for it *was* democracy. Today most sports played by children are played in the company of adults—organized by adults, supervised by adults, watched by adults. Often they seem to be more for the benefit of adults than for the children. I have watched soccer games where the parent audience—jumping up and down and screaming curses at their own children and everyone else's—were burning more calories than their bored and listless offspring. But even when parents are reasonable and coaches don't act as if losing a game would cost them their job, organized sports of this kind do nothing to prepare children to live in a democratic society. The children don't make rules, don't negotiate terms, don't resolve conflicts. All this is done by adults. The children might reasonably come to feel that making rules has nothing to do with them. All they are learning to do is to obey authority. It might not be too much to say, they are learning voter apathy.

There are, of course, places where children still play together unsupervised. Perhaps this is why skateboarding has loomed so large as a symbol of intergenerational antagonism. Skateboarding is one of the few places where children still organize their own play and set their own rules and standards. Their slogan, "skateboarding is not a crime," is an ironic reflection of the fact that it is an "outlaw" sport—one that lies outside the orderly sphere of adult control.

One of the reasons childhood is valued in democratic societies is that children are uncommitted to the status quo. They are not even entirely familiar with it; they ask naive questions about why things are the way they are—questions that often amuse adults, who usually accept "the way things are" without thinking about them overmuch. Adults see their proper role as one of inculcating whatever social idiocies happen to be operative at the moment, and they are usually successful in ridding their children of the clear vision they started with. But there is always a certain amount of slippage in this process. Sometimes the answers are unconvincing, and the child grows to adulthood with the vision of a better future. Anderson's tale, "The Emperor's New Clothes," in which only a small child sees that the Emperor is in fact naked, perfectly captures the essential relationship between political and familial democracy.

Children are naturally imaginative, and this is another reason why they are so essential to the future of a democratic society. They can envision things being different from the way they are—a vision often lost by adults ground down by everyday "realities." But imagination in today's children is in danger of being smothered by constant commercialized input. Children's toys, for example, used to be generic, allowing the child to invest them with meaning and clothe them with stories. Children today are bombarded with spin-off toys already fitted out with manufactured personalities, prefabricated adventures, and a host of required accessories so that imagination plays little or no part. Children are, in effect, instructed how to play.

Television has the same effect. Books and radio shows demanded use of the imagination to flesh out the limited stimuli presented to the reader or listener, but TV demands nothing. Everything is laid out for the viewer in living color, and the imaginations of children who spend large amounts of time in front of it tend to atrophy. TV seems to sap the capacity to imagine situations never actually encountered.

A recent incident made me newly aware of this. A group of young actors rehearsing a play of mine were puzzled by the play's premise, which involved human inmates in a zoo. The idea was not particularly original (a novella written in the 1920s adopted the same premise, and a zoo in Denmark actually features such an item). I was using the metaphor to say something about how ordinary people deal with hierarchies and the constraints of what Erving Goffman called total institutions.[1] But the actors asked a number of questions that seemed surprisingly literal and were only satisfied when they decided the play was "like one of those *Twilight Zone* episodes from the '50s." Yet there was no element of horror or the supernatural in the play; aside from the metaphor of its premise, the play was more or less realistic.

But the experience was a familiar one. It reminded me of how often students had expressed puzzlement over some fantastic event in a play or novel because they assumed it had to be autobiographical, and of the times I had run up against blank youthful stares by saying something only mildly fanciful. It is as if an unusual idea can be grasped only if it can be linked to something already encountered on the TV screen.

Perhaps this is the reason for the fascination with "Real TV" and "Docudramas"; for the plundering of classics, comic books, and current events for ideas; for the plethora of sequels, prequels, and revivals; for the fact that even in the realm of science fiction—traditionally an area where imagination has been king—most movie and TV plots are mere extrapolations of present realities or tired retreads of Cold War material. One can't help feeling that the entertainment industry is in desperate need of a new idea.

Yet although the pool may be diminishing, there are still plenty of young people out there with vivid imaginations and the artistic ability to produce superior creative material. Prophets of doom have had a low success rate over the years, usually by underestimating human resiliency. However much we herd young children around from one adult-supervised activity to another, they still manage to find islands of independence, and no doubt always will.

My youngest daughter, when she was six, begged for a much-advertised doll that could speak, cry, be fed, and sit up in its crib. We argued in vain that such toys are never of interest for long, and finally decided to let her discover their vacuity for herself, which she soon did, and it was quickly cast aside. But one day, many months later, hearing a strange grinding sound and shrieks of childish laughter coming from her room, we discovered that she and a friend had retrieved the doll, tied it down in its crib, and activated the mechanism to make it sit up, creating an impasse that was both dramatic and extremely comical.

Although immigration today is only a trickle relative to the huge influxes of the late nineteenth and early twentieth centuries, it has never ceased to be of huge symbolic importance to Americans. All through this century Americans have been virulently hostile to new arrivals while expressing great fascination with those who arrived a generation or two before.

Every nation needs a past—some kind of core experience that will help people define who they are. Americans seek this with a desperation that perhaps reflects their inherent poverty in this regard. Except for Native Americans, everyone came here from some other place—a place with rich traditions of its own. American artists and writers are continually looking for "roots"—for a way to build a cultural essence of some kind. They look to the small Midwestern town of 1910 or the New England village of 1750 or the Old West, but none of these symbols seems to stick, perhaps because all represent such a minute fragment of what it means to be American.

Yet there has never been a time when the struggles of immigrants have failed to fascinate us. It doesn't seem to matter what their particular background is—Irish, Italian, Jewish, Asian, Latino—these are the stories that make the best-seller lists. Why is it that we so easily identify with these experiences, no matter how far they might be removed from our own? Why do white Americans become so absorbed in *Roots* or *The Joy Luck Club*? Because we are all "second generation" in one way or another. Even Native Americans have intergenerational, culture-clash experiences. We all know what it is to be different from our parents—to live in a world different from theirs. *To be an immigrant is to be more truly American than to be born here*. When we come to recognize this essential fact of our national heritage, we will have truly matured as a nation.

Technology now drives the wedge between generations—computers being the latest phenomenon giving children an edge over their parents. One additional irony since this book was written is that our attitudes toward technology have also changed: even though children are better adapted to our technological world than their parents, they are also more cynical about its claimed advantages.

In the first edition I said that when centralized, authoritarian regimes attack the family, they undermine themselves by creating a child-oriented populace that questions parental (and therefore all) authority. This has had its predicted effect in the former Soviet Union and is beginning to have the same result in China.

When democracy prevails in China it will be due in part to the Cultural Revolution—that disastrous onslaught on Chinese tradition instigated by Mao in the late sixties. The Red Guards delivered a crushing blow to millennia of slavish subservience, and while most Chinese look back on the Guards' brutal rampages with justified horror it had a profound and lasting impact. The Tiananmen Square uprising—regardless of the profound ideological differences—is a direct descendent of the Cultural Revolution in its questioning of tradition, of elders, of authority. It was the first premature bud of an inevitable spring.

We think of Tiananmen Square only as a failure—the crushing of democracy. But every major change begins with failures—a defeated program, an aborted coup, a crushed rebellion, an atrocity, martyrs. We are a media-driven people with a very short attention span; long-term trends tend to elude us. Consider the amazing fact that modern computer programs failed even to anticipate the year 2000!

I once participated in a panel discussion with journalist Morley Safer, conservative commentator Ben Wattenberg, anthropologist Ashley Montague, and the late poet Allen Ginsberg. At one point in the hopelessly muddled discussion, Allen suggested that our confusion was due to the fact that we were operating with different time frames. "Morley and Ben," he said, "are thinking in terms of the next six months. Ashley is thinking in terms of three hundred years, Phil in terms of three thousand years, and I'm thinking in terms of eternity!"

Democratization in China will not occur in six months, but neither will it take hundreds or thousands of years. Barring a major war it can be expected to have reached European levels within two or three decades, for the simple reason that economic development cannot keep pace without it.

———●———

In the first chapter we suggested that democracy was an institution that increased the power and availability of individuals uncommitted to the status quo. We also argued that democratic response patterns are learned in the family. In this chapter I would like to explore both of these questions in greater detail, since taken together they have some rather surprising implications.

Our society is geared to the assumption that little in it is permanent, save for a few values so ambiguous as to have no effect on behavior. But if change is truly chronic it becomes itself a stable condition, and must therefore depend upon factors that are unchanging. We are so attuned to the changes that we often overlook the stable conditions upon which they depend.

One of these stable institutions I have called the "democratic family," by which I mean simply a family system in which the social distance between parent and child is relatively small, the exercise of parental authority is relatively mild, and the child tends not to be seen as a mere parental possession without independent legal status. It is, in other words, the system that presently obtains in our own middle class and toward which most of the Western world seems to be moving. I would like to discuss first the sources and then the consequences of this system.

In Chapter One we cited evidence showing that an autocratic, centralized system of communication was most efficient only for simple tasks under static conditions, but that for adaptability to changing conditions, for the solution of complex and ambiguous problems requiring rapid adoption of new ideas, a decentralized, equalitarian system was superior. One of the reasons for the inferiority of the autocratic condition was that the decision maker was likely to discard a crucial, innovating idea because it seemed impractical or he was too busy.[2] He was committed, in other words, to the current system with its pressures and rewards.

This is merely one of many illustrations of the fact that evolution (biological as well as cultural) proceeds in a kind of leapfrog fashion: bold new advances do not typically occur in those groups currently in the vanguard of development.[3] The advanced cultures and advantaged groups are too embroiled in the success of their current *modus operandi* to be available for new departures. It is those societies (or those groups within a society) with nothing to lose by change—nothing invested in today—that can exploit the radically new opportunity.[4]

But there is a flaw in this reasoning. If democracy makes the uncommitted more available and powerful, does this not itself commit them? If we raise the position of any group in a society, do they not thereby *acquire* a vested interest in the status quo? If so, then democratization is a self-extinguishing mechanism.

This is why the democratic family is the most potent expression of democracy, and a necessary condition for its survival. For the young are, by their very nature, uncommitted. They constitute the only group that can perpetually renew its lack of commitment as its older members are siphoned off into the ranks of the committed. The only status quo in which youth *as a whole* acquires a vested interest is the democratic family itself. This is what I mean when I talk of change being chronic and say that this chronic change depends upon a stable and permanent condition. The democratic family assigns high status to a group that has no commitment to any specific item in the culture other than its accent on youth. It thus maximizes the possibility for exploitation of new opportunities.

An interesting precursor of the democratic family is primogeniture. This is a compromise institution that realizes many of the advantages of both the democratic and authoritarian family systems. The eldest son exploits existing conditions, while the younger, who has no vested interest in the status quo, provides the raw material for social change. For the most part this hedge against the future is pure waste, like its biological analogue the mutation. Yet under certain conditions it may mean the difference between survival and decay, as it probably did for eighteenth-century England. Its power is enhanced if the younger son is given some kind of special status, as in Japan. William Goode comments on the fact that younger sons in Japan are more indulged and allowed more freedom, since "in Japanese folk wisdom, it is the younger sons who are the innovators."[5]

The democratic family extends this approach to all children in the family. It assumes that children may adapt better to their environment than did their parents, and that therefore their parents cannot take for granted the superiority of their own knowledge, perceptions, attitudes, and skills. Thus it not only causes but can only exist under conditions of chronic change. The democratic family is based on an expectation that tomorrow will be different from today, and that there is, hence, some ambiguity as to how to socialize the child. "Socialization for what?" is its fundamental question.

Norman Ryder showed how closely social change is tied to age "cohorts"—classes of individuals who have simultaneously experienced some new set of historical social conditions at an important period in their lives, or have newly eluded such conditions.[6] We commonly use the term *generation* rather than *cohort*, but it is at best an awkward device, since it implies discrete lumps of individuals twenty-five years or so apart when, in fact, people are being born continuously. Furthermore, the rate of social change has increased so much that we can identify many different cohorts within any twenty-five-year period. One could once speak in a leisurely fashion about "the lost generation," or "the war generation," but in the last decade or so the mass media have paraded half a dozen or more generations before us. While a more precise term than *generation* would have been useful fifty years ago, I suspect it is significant that it was advanced only recently, just at the point when *generation* began to refer to the brief ascendancy of rock-and-roll stars (whose fans are increasingly a specific cohort with whom they age together). The image makers have, in the meantime, despaired and taken refuge in the portmanteau term, "the *now* generation."

This increase in the number of identifiable cohorts means that two things are happening: (1) social change is occurring so rapidly that every few years individuals at a given stage in the life cycle are experiencing a somewhat different social environment; and (2) something is making these individuals susceptible to the influence of such changes. This is a circular process—the more susceptible, the faster the change; the faster the change, the more susceptible. In this way the rate of change constantly accelerates in a spiral fashion.

The democratic family is a key link in this circular chain. By raising the status of the child, lessening the social distance between child and parent, and reducing the role of parental authority, the child's susceptibility to the immediate social environment is increased, while his susceptibility to tradition is decreased. But the democratic family is a result as well as a cause of change acceleration, for any increase in the rate of social change tends also to increase the parents' doubt about their own values and customs, and to make them view their children as better adapted to the world they will grow into than the parents themselves.[7]

But how is such a cycle set in motion in the first place? Is it something internal to the structure of families that begins it, or some outside force? The most likely answer is that some sudden external, accidental, but overwhelming change in the social environment produces what Ryder calls an "experiential chasm" between age cohorts—particularly between parents and children. Such chasms serve to invalidate parental authority and the pertinence of parental wisdom, for the parents have not even experienced what is of central importance to the child, or at least have not experienced it in the same way, at the same time of life.

In most cases such events—an unprecedented climatic disaster, for example, or an invasion by unfamiliar warrior nomads—are temporary disturbances. They are somehow integrated into a new pattern, which is just as stable and enduring as the old. Parental authority is invalidated only for that generation which was unable to anticipate the crisis, and it soon reestablishes itself. But what if the community or society receives several such shocks in succession? Change then becomes an expectation, tradition irrelevant, and the democratic family obtains a foothold. As Ryder observes: "The products of earlier education become debris that chokes off later growth"; and major environmental changes enhance the importance of such growth.[8] Two examples will serve to illustrate the role of environmental disturbances in transforming parental wisdom into "debris."

The Jewish Immigrant

My first example is the impact of immigration on the family system of the Jewish *shtetl*. It illustrates again the advantageous position of the uncommitted under conditions of rapid social change.[9]

Any persecuted minority group must in some way cope with the fact that its position impairs the viability of the male role. Protecting and providing may not be universal masculine attributes, but when the larger community in which the minority is embedded defines the role in this way, the minority group males will tend to appear less adequate. This has been a serious problem for the black male, as many observers have noted. For Eastern European Jews living in the *shtetl* (and I would prefer to restrict my analysis to this group, even though much of what I have to say can be more broadly applied), an interesting if only partly successful solution to this dilemma emerged from centuries of persecution. Masculine status was attached to learning—a learning that was essential in that it concerned the core and focus of the culture, but rather irrelevant to worldly issues not tied to human relationships within that culture. It was an ingenious solution, making a virtue of a necessity and creating a practicality (that is, the moral and legal problems created by the confrontation of ancient laws and current realities) where none had existed. The man with the highest status was not only the most learned but also the most withdrawn from worldly activities and insulated from daily contact with the hostile majority.[10] Insofar as everyday life was dominated by religious law, this statement must be qualified, but the learned man did not concern himself with the business of making a living and protecting his family from harm. These more practical issues were left to his wife and to God, which in practice often meant gentile police, firemen, and soldiers.[11] It was the woman who managed and often earned the money, who bought and sold, who bargained with peasants and spoke the local language, acting as a buffer against the world for her sheltered husband.

This pattern was not maintained without strain. The women could not carry so great a share of the burdens of life and still be altogether comfortable with the submissive feminine ideal. They were conscious of the extent to which they were mothers to their husbands, although their protest was limited to irony (such as referring to the husband as "my breadwinner").[12]

For the *prosteh yidn* or common people this pattern was less marked. Men as well as women were realists and hustlers, and there was less sexual segregation, a less rigid sexual division of labor, and a tendency toward freer choice in marriage.[13] When it came to emigration, then, it would be the *prosteh yidn* and the women who would have least to lose in terms of status, who would be best adapted to transact successfully the difficulties of the journey, and who would find themselves most at home in the new environment. The knowledge and skills of the learned Jew would be essentially useless unless and until he could be transplanted into a complete new ghetto. But the more permeable nature of the new society, which both demanded and offered new occupational roles, upset the old balance, and made the position of the learned Jew somewhat difficult to reestablish. The ideal of learning became diluted with practicality, so that highest status went to the lawyer or doctor. The brittle patriarchy in the family collapsed utterly.[14]

Thus it was those least committed to the old cultural pattern who were best able to turn the new environment to their advantage—to seize and mold a new pattern under new conditions. For Jews emigrating from the *shtetl* the availability of the uncommitted was an accidental goodness of fit. The democratic family system translates such accidents into a prevailing certainty by insulating the young from the committed, minimizing the prestige of adults, and building segregated worlds of childhood and adolescence.

The Manus

My second example is unusual in that it involves a democratic family system where we would least expect it—in a remote New Guinea island inhabited by nonliterate Melanesians. We cannot answer the question as to how such a system ever emerged in such an unlikely place—the causes are lost forever in unrecorded history.

The Manus were first studied by Margaret Mead in 1928, at which time she commented at length on the contrast between their permissive child-rearing practices and the prudish, materialistic, ascetic, industrious, business-oriented quality of adult life—a combination not dissimilar to our own culture. She returned to the Manus in 1953, "because I had heard that they had changed more remarkably and more drastically than any other of the peoples of the Pacific."[15]

Mead's earlier description of the Manus' approach to child-rearing is like a caricature of our own. Although adult males were engaged in "unremitting labor" directed toward the accumulation of property, these same fathers made no demands whatever upon their children outside of prudery and respect for property. They were not taught anything about the complexities of adult life and objected to being bothered about them. "Property, morality, and security for the next generation" were the concerns of the adults, but the children did as they pleased, bullying and tyrannizing over their parents. Obedience and deference were unknown, and children ate and slept and played when and where they wished, despite their parents' futile pleading. They were never asked to give anything up for their parents and often shouted contemptuous obscenities at them. They lived in their own world—a cooperative, sharing one that had no relationship to the competitive, property-centered world of the adults. Yet when they reached adolescence they moved painfully from this happy, irresponsible existence onto the bottom rung of the adult economic ladder, partaking in the adult quarrels they had treated with such indifference, abandoning their world of friendship for one in which friendliness detached from economic considerations was almost impossible. As children they were bright and inquisitive but unimaginative and hostile to make-believe. Since young boys spent almost no time with adults, they knew nothing of the social organization of their own society until they became adults themselves.[16]

We do not know whether this was a stable pattern or whether change was already taking place when Mead first studied the Manus. But between Mead's first and second visits a rather cataclysmic environmental change occurred: during World War II more than a million Americans occupied the Admiralty Islands. The Manus, who prior to this time had encountered only small groups of colonial rulers, had an opportunity to experience (in a dazzling if somewhat distorted form) Western culture to the full. In response to this experience the Manus consciously and deliberately discarded the bulk of their old culture, particularly its more inconvenient and burdensome aspects, and adopted a new one. They destroyed their household "ghosts," relocated their village, abolished taboos and avoidances, rearranged their economic system, and (against the resistance of the colonial authorities) tried to establish broader political cooperation.[17]

The Manus in 1928 were in no way less primitive or superstitious than their neighbors, although their culture was unique in its child-orientation and its insulation of children from adult life. In their "New Way" they drew not only upon their experiences with an alien culture, but also upon the social patterns of their childhood peer groups. This child-adult discontinuity provided a ready-made lever for change. The Manus' willingness to protect children from the burdens of the present was easily translated into the idea that the children constitute the best hope for a better future society.[18] The fact that the Manus of 1928 did not provide their children with an education that would, in Ryder's terms, become "debris," gave their society an advantage over other Pacific cultures.

This idea helps us to understand the "cargo cult" phenomenon, which has occurred so frequently since World War II. Its usual form is a kind of religious frenzy that sweeps over an area, sparked by a prophet who persuades everyone to destroy all his possessions to make room for the Second Coming of American cargo ships bringing all the trappings of Western culture. Westerners typically look upon it with indulgent condescension, as another example of how primitive irrationality can lead to disaster. If our argument is correct, however, the cargo cult response is a rational act of commitment to change. It takes a bit of frenzy to say "out with the old and in with the new" in quite such total terms—to reject one's whole way of life in favor of a distant and uncertain possibility. But if the change is desired, the first necessary act is the destruction of the "debris that chokes off later growth." This destruction is unwise in the sense that the ships will not come. But it is sociologically wise in that they have placed themselves in a state of readiness for the Western culture that they ardently desire. As Mead points out, it is easier to embrace a new culture in its entirety—since it is a meaningful, integrated whole—than to try to splice two cultures together. Substituting clothes for grass skirts (to use Mead's own example) without introducing soap and chairs produces dirt and disease; without sewing machines, starch, and irons, it creates a society of ragamuffins; without closets, it produces huts that are cluttered with hanging clothes, and so on. As Mead points out it is easier for a Samoan to become a New Yorker than to become a half-acculturated (or deculturated) Samoan.[19] The cargo cultists seem at some level to have recognized a truth that has eluded Western colonialists for centuries. Only their premise—the wish to embrace Western culture—can be called irrational. Once this goal is accepted, the steps they have taken toward it are the only ones that are both rational and possible for them. They have freed themselves from any commitment to the past.

The democratic family is a pattern that, through its insulation of childhood from adult tradition, contains a small, built-in cargo cult experience for each cohort.

The American Family

The best example of how a democratic family system comes into being is found in our own history. Here four related but distinguishable historical forces interacted to produce and sustain a family pattern that was altogether unintended and is still under frequent attack, although it is far too firmly entrenched now to be dislodged by anything short of a world cataclysm. Each of these forces—the transplantation of the original settlers, the Western frontier, the great immigrations of the nineteenth and early twentieth centuries, and the profound technological changes of the past one hundred years—drove an experiential chasm between parent and child, which eroded the authoritarian family pattern prevailing in Europe.

Some people imagine the democratic family to be of very recent origin—emerging full-blown from Victorian patriarchy. There is no evidence, however, to support the idea that an authoritarian family system ever existed on American soil as a widespread social pattern. Individual families of this kind always have and always will exist. Small groups and subcultures may have maintained an authoritarian pattern for a brief period. Moralists have been advocating parental severity since the first boat landed. But as nearly as we can tell, the democratic family began to prevail throughout the American colonies within a generation or two following the first settlements, and, as we shall see, has never been seriously challenged. William Goode points out that when we attempt to track down what he calls "the classical family of Western nostalgia," it keeps receding into the mists of ancestral reminiscence.[20] Every generation is certain it once existed but none seem actually to have experienced it.

We would expect that whenever and wherever the rate of change decelerates, the democratic family should decay and a more authoritarian pattern emerge. What seems unique to the American situation is the concatenation of forces that have successfully and repeatedly reversed this process of deceleration. Despite the efforts of Puritan moralists, the continual replenishment of American life with European families (with European assumptions), and the gradual aging and stabilizing of the society, the authoritarian family has been repeatedly deracinated whenever it threatened to take hold.

The First Settlers

The beginnings of the democratic family in the United States can be located in the experiential chasm established between the first generation of native-born settlers and their European-born parents. Oscar Handlin describes vividly the many ways in which these children were better adapted to their environment than their parents. To the European-born settler, for example, the forest never ceased to be a dangerous and magical place, filled with supernatural beings of malevolent intent. But to the native-born child it was simply his backyard, a comfortable and interesting place in which to run about. The vast European pantheon of wood spirits barely survived the voyage and were never to establish significant colonies on American shores. With few exceptions, our woodlands have remained supernatural deserts, lonely and uninteresting in comparison with their European counterparts. The example may seem trivial, but it is one of many such differences.

Most writers stress the role of economic factors in bringing about the democratization of the American family—the dependence of the male on wife and children for survival in the wilderness. But similar dependence can be found elsewhere without the democratic family, and while it may be a necessary condition, it clearly cannot be a sufficient one.[21] What seems crucial is the irrelevance of so much of parental knowledge for the successful adaptation of the child, often accompanied by explicit parental hopes for the child's social mobility. Indeed, who could teach the other more about living in the wilderness, parent or child?

The Frontier

What was true for the first settlers remained true on the Western frontier as long as it existed. As the terrain changed, the qualities necessary for successful adaptation changed, and the child continued to teach the parent the ways of the world.

This is perhaps the real basis of Frederick Jackson Turner's argument that the frontier was a perennial democratizing force in American society.[22] The frontier may have been only one instance of the frenetic mobility that George Pierson sees as the essence of our culture,[23] but this does not deny the importance of Turner's argument. While there were other springs to the democratic impulse, the frontier was a major source of radical democracy as long as it survived. Above all, it helped maintain the democratic family as a dominant form in American life. As Calhoun observed, "'For the children' was the motto of many a pioneer, who endured the wilderness hardships that the next generation might have a better chance."

Yet what of conditions in the East? Did the democratic family atrophy there with the passage of time and increasing stabilization? This is a difficult question to answer. If we use the exhortations of native moralists as evidence that the conditions they are trying to create already exist, then the authoritarian family has prevailed in America from the early seventeenth century to the present. But if we use the reports of foreign visitors—surely a more objective index—then we must conclude that the American family has always been equalitarian, permissive, and child-oriented relative to its European counterparts.[24] At every period in American history statements are made by foreign visitors that American children are treated as equals and friends by their parents, that they are never punished or disciplined, that their parents indulge them and are constantly concerned about their needs and wishes, that they are allowed to intrude upon adult activities, and so on. Even the restrained de Tocqueville was moved to remark that in America "the family, in the Roman and aristocratic signification of the word, does not exist."[25]

The Myth of the Authoritarian Past

Throughout Calhoun's history of the American family, he speaks of the decay of authoritarianism in the parent-child relationship as if it occurred anew in each generation. He also claims that democratization was less pronounced in parts of New England and the South.[26] Yet, these finer distinctions receive little emphasis in the report of travelers and the complaints of natives. The mildness of parental authority and the independence and omnipresence of children are attributed by foreigners to all classes and regions. Many authors have documented this consistency of European comment on familial democracy in America, and there is no need to duplicate their efforts here.[27] But the curious tendency for native Americans to perceive this chronic condition as a new phenomenon deserves brief attention. For example, in the 1830s and 1840s—the supposed heyday of the belief in "breaking the will"[28]—an educational journal comments on the *new* cult of childhood as something duplicated only in the classical age; a physician attacks the "growing view" that punishment is unnecessary in child-rearing; and a man complains that he grew up in an age when the child was nothing and reached maturity in a period when it was everything.[29] And in 1869, when the patriarchal family was supposedly flourishing, we find a writer complaining of its disappearance—note how little the fantasy he cherished has changed in a hundred years: "the father at the head of the board with his wife and twelve stalwart sons about him, and with the aged grandsire and grandame in the corner."[30] Calhoun himself, with a fine disregard for his own first two volumes, views the nation in 1900 as entering on the "century of the child," again during a period popularly regarded now as particularly authoritarian.[31] He comments on the decline of moral tales in children's literature, notes that because of the absence of a nursery the children are allowed to "tear all over the house," and suggests that "the best American homes have come to center in the child." These comments, however, are interspersed with quotations drawn from the 1860s that refer to the same phenomena.[32] Finally, we note with interest that "one reason Americans are not strenuous in discipline is that coercion is supposed to break the will and hinder self-expression"— an attitude that we usually attribute to Freud's influence and that is supposed to have first made its appearance in the 1930s. Actually, it is mentioned as a parental motive by travelers throughout the eighteenth and nineteenth centuries, usually accompanied by the equally familiar argument that such a policy results in the American child's becoming a dictator in the home.[33]

It seems hazardous, therefore, to claim any gross changes in parental authority patterns in America during the past three centuries. Clergymen and physicians may have exerted authoritarian pressures at one time or another, and the emergence of large family fortunes and pseudo-aristocratic traditions may have given a toehold to familial authoritarianism in the more settled sections of the country during the nineteenth century; but, if so, the trend was not strong enough to cause so much as a ripple in the stream of foreign commentary on the American family. If there was an authoritarian threat it did not succeed but was soon overwhelmed by new pressures for change and forced to take refuge, like the losing tribe in some ancient invasion, in whatever small and undesired pockets and corners were left to it by the victors. The myth of the authoritarian family of yore has probably never lacked for a few real-life models here and there, but fundamentally it merely expresses the fact that a child is unaware of living in a child-oriented household, but is sharply cognizant of whatever restrictions *are* placed on him; this bias is reversed when he becomes a parent, and he then imagines a change to have occurred.

The Puritan Dilemma

Curiously, what seemed to be the very strongholds of familial authoritarianism often proved later to be the springs of its demise. The most important example of this is the Puritan family, usually regarded as the foundation of the old-fashioned American family. A great deal of nonsense has been written, and even more assumed, about this chapter in the history of the American family. The worst error has been to equate the aspirations and precepts of a few divines with the practices of the population at large, which is like equating the social life of the late-fifteenth-century Florentines with the exhortations of Savonarola. We have no evidence to indicate that the Puritan fathers were any more successful in imposing an authoritarian family system than they were in abolishing the casual sexual customs of the rank-and-file colonist. Complaints about the rebelliousness and disrespectfulness of youth and the generality of fornication and adultery are equally pervasive throughout the early Colonial period, and while there is no reason to assume that the actual behavior in either category was more conspicuous than in our own era, there is equally little reason for assuming it to have been less so.[34] My purpose here, however, is not to assess the efficacy of Puritan repressiveness on either front, but to show that Puritan efforts to legislate family relationships had the unintended consequence of contributing to the democratization of the family—a process that is of the utmost relevance to the comparable efforts of the revolutionary governments of the twentieth century.

We know, of course, that the manifest intent of the Puritan divines was quite different, that their image of the proper family was a highly authoritarian one. God was viewed as an absolute ruler, and the Fifth Commandment was to be the governing principle of all human relationships, with the father receiving respect, submission, and obedience from wife, children, and servants alike. Independence and initiative, far from being encouraged, were viewed as expressions of sinful or heretical proclivities.[35]

I would like to offer the hypothesis, however, that *any* nonfamily-based collectivity (I am excluding kinship organizations) that intervenes between parent and child and attempts to regulate and modify the parent-child relationship *will have a democratizing impact on that relationship regardless of its intent.* For however much the state or community may wish to inculcate obedience and submission in the child, its intervention betrays (1) a lack of confidence in the only objects from whom a small child can learn authoritarian submission, the parents, and (2) an overweening interest in the future development of the child—in other words, a child-centered orientation.

Edmund Morgan places great emphasis on Puritan intervention in the parent-child relationship. He points out the many regulations protecting family members from each other, the great concern that children be properly educated, and the willingness to remove the child from the family should the parents fall short of community requirements. Like the founders of the kibbutzim in Israel, the Puritans saw child development as a community issue first and an individual or family issue second. This priority was expressed in the view that loyalty, affection, and submission to a husband or father should always be kept in careful subordination to corresponding sentiments toward God.[36]

Similarly, although the Puritans had no intention of encouraging self-expression or individuality in their children, their child-centeredness set severe limits on the exercise of parental authority. They were opposed to corporal punishment except in what they considered to be extreme situations, since they viewed punishment as purificatory rather than educative. Children were to be trained with due attention to their individual peculiarities rather than by a general formula. Marriages were to be contracted with the voluntary agreement of the principals, since a coerced match might prevent the couple from carrying out their obligation to love each other. Nor should a son be forced into an occupation against his will, since this might violate his particular "calling" and prevent him from serving God in the way he was best able.[37]

This preoccupation with the *internal* development of the child betrays the degree to which the Puritans had already been captured by the worldly future-orientation that has always dominated our culture. One sees them frequently struggling with this contradiction between (1) a theology which purports to know the only true course to be followed, and hence need brook no questioning or opposition, and (2) the ambiguous physical and social environment, adaptation to which required unknown faculties and skills, perhaps lying nearer at hand to the young than to the old. The injunction to observe the child's proclivities before attempting to train it, and the reluctance to force a marriage or a career against the child's will, express a rivulet of parental self-doubt, which was to become a torrent in the ensuing centuries. Indeed, it is Morgan's thesis that the child-orientation of the Puritans is what ultimately undid them. Of particular interest is his remark that "by the latter half of the seventeenth century it had become an accepted tradition that the founders of New England had left the old world for the sake of their children"—primarily to protect them from evil influences.[38] While these motives may actually have been unimportant, it is significant that the Puritan fathers should so quickly have placed themselves in the same category as modern suburbanites, who also exile themselves from the centers of their culture in order to protect their children from noxious influence and ensure their future development.

The growth of a child-centered orientation, however, was less important in undermining parental authority than the effect of community intervention itself. The Puritans, to be sure, saw themselves as bolstering rather than undermining parental authority, and their behavior largely substantiates this view: this was no revolutionary attempt to set up the state or the local community *in loco parentis*. Yet at the same time the Puritan community was more than an extension of parental authority onto a higher plane, like the village elder or clan head. These continue and enlarge rather than oppose parental authority, but the Puritan divines saw themselves as representing the authority of God, and saw this authority as *competitive* with parental authority in the last analysis. The Puritans did every-thing possible to de-emphasize this conflict, but it appeared often in their discussions of familial affection. The child was told again and again, apparently with great effect, that love of parents, if too strong, constituted idolatry—that it must always be subordinated to love of God. Hence an element of choice was introduced: one could more easily apportion one's submissive and rebellious feelings to the disadvantage of temporal authority without feeling guilt. This choice was not unique to the Puritans, and is only one visible link in the long chain of increasing pluralism in our society. What is important in it is the establishment of the community's indepen-dent claim on the child's future.

The significance of this claim is illuminated by Philippe Ariès's brilliant analysis of the changing role of the child from the Renais-sance to the present day. Ariès points out that the concept of child-hood as a separate period of life with special characteristics is relatively modern. A few centuries ago a child was simply a small adult, wearing the same clothing, engaged in the same activities, acting on the same assumptions as adults. He was in no way set apart or shielded from adult society as children are today, with pur-suits and interests specific to their age.[39] This change corresponds to the growth of an investment by the community in the child's future. One segregates children from adult life because one wishes to do something special with them—to effect some kind of social change or to adapt to one. Such segregation insulates the child from the social patterns of the present and makes him more recep-tive to some envisioned future. In Ryder's terms, the concept of childhood as a special period of life helps to increase the experi-ential chasm between cohorts and to make future cohorts more malleable and plastic. This is what Ariès means when he says that medieval civilization lacked a concept of transition between child-hood and adulthood, a transition now represented by formal edu-cation. Ariès calls it, quite appropriately, a quarantine. We might also liken it to the current fantasies about deep-freezing one's body until the cures for its diseases are invented. "Family and school together removed the child from adult society," making him amenable to influences which might change the nature of his later adult behavior.[40]

A future orientation—perhaps but not necessarily associated with a utopian ideology—a desire to manipulate the child-rearing process to further community goals, a consequent confrontation between the community and the parent for the child's allegiance: these are the bases of a child-centered society and a democratic family system. The child emerges as the receptacle for future hopes, and hence bears a higher status than his elders, whose authority is weakened by its doubtful relevance to this future and uncertain conformity to the standards thereof.[41] When this condition is achieved, the rate of social change is accelerated—or more precisely, the gravitational forces which retard change are weakened—and the process becomes self-perpetuating.

The Great Immigration

But let us now return to the American family. I have argued that a barrage of forces creating experiential chasms prevented the authoritarian family from gaining a secure foothold on American soil. The first was the impact of the wilderness on the original settlers, the second the ever-moving frontier. We have even seen how one authoritarian force, Puritan ideology, actually contained within itself the seeds of familial democracy and was hence powerless to resist, and indeed, to some extent, even expressed the forces tending toward democratization.

The third blow to authoritarianism was the sudden influx, in the latter half of the nineteenth century, of new immigrants in increasing numbers and from increasingly alien cultures. It is almost as if fate had conspired to maintain a constant democratizing pressure, for immigration increased precisely as the frontier receded, and the degree of cultural shock experienced by the immigrants (supplied more and more by regions with cultures less and less like the prevailing Anglo-Saxon norm) also increased as the shock effect of frontier life diminished.

American literature is rich in descriptions of the chasm between first- and second-generation immigrants: the child who is more acculturated than the parents and can act as an interpreter, the child who is a repository of parental hopes for social advancement but also an object of parental resentment for his rebellion against old-world culture and parental authority. There are two points seldom made about this drama, however. The first is that without the development of the "quarantined" childhood that Ariès discusses, the acculturation of the child could not and would not have occurred. Immigration itself would not have created a chasm of such magnitude had the child instantly participated in the adult life of the transplanted community. It required, in addition, the exposure of the child to the insulated life of the age-segregated school and play group.

The second point is that this experience of the immigrant is not a foreigner's experience but an American experience. There has never been a time when a child was not better adapted than his parents to live in American society, when he was not the bearer of aspirations for a better future. What the immigrant imagined to be a problem peculiar to his foreign status was really an ironic initiation into American life.

There is additional irony in the fact that the newcomers brought with them a far more authoritarian family system than that prevailing here, and concentrated themselves in precisely those settled areas that might be expected to be most vulnerable to authoritarianism. Yet the net result of this infusion was further democratization. For although new pockets of familial authoritarianism did develop in unassimilated ghettos, those individuals who were able to enter the mainstream of American culture had to reject their parents all the more strongly. Social mobility always produces an experiential chasm, even without an immigrant background. But since the immigrants typically began in poverty, assimilation and social mobility tended to occur simultaneously. Thus the price of entry into the American middle class was the pulverization of those conditions that nourish the authoritarian family. Paradoxically, the very existence of these pockets of familial authoritarianism served to heighten and dramatize the initiation process.

Technological Change

The constancy of environmental pressure toward family democracy in American society is, in retrospect, an object of wonder. For just as the tide of immigration was suddenly and permanently dammed, the fourth and most powerful force for democratization reached maturity. This force was technological change, and unlike the earlier ones, it has no natural limits. By World War I it had accelerated to the point where a disruptive invention could be counted on at least every twenty years, and it was driving wedges between cohorts fast enough to outmode parental assumptions before the child-rearing process was completed. Like the earlier colonists, frontiersmen, and non-English-speaking immigrants, *all* Americans of the present century must face the irrelevance of their knowledge and skills for the world into which their children will mature. And this is an accelerating trend. It is not merely that parents cannot help their children with math and science problems, or that the children accept easily inventions that their parents still find a little mysterious or disconcerting. It is that parents cannot define the parameters of the future for their children—cannot even establish the terms of possible change or a range of alternative outcomes. They are therefore useless and obsolete in a way that rarely befell parents of any previous century.

If this view is correct we can predict that another hundred years or so will find the democratic family ensconced everywhere on the globe, barring nuclear disaster or some major deceleration in the rate of technological change and diffusion. Such a prediction, however, is bolstered by a fifth and somewhat less impersonal factor to which we may now turn.

The State and the Family

I have argued that familial democratization in America resulted from a series of environmental forces that widened the experiential chasm between parent and child. Only once, during our discussion of the Puritans, was there a hint of public policy, and the consequences of this were portrayed as unintended. I suggested then that any community intervention between parent and child would tend to produce familial democracy regardless of its intent. This argument becomes more significant when we survey the less-industrialized segments of the world today, their aspirations and the models of change available to them. By this I mean that it would now be difficult to find an underdeveloped country that would be satisfied with the kind of gradual, spontaneous industrialization experienced by England and the United States during the nineteenth century. What is desired is a rapid and forced crash program that will close the enormous gaps that presently exist. For this the models are the Soviet Union and China—models that include the centralization of power necessary to coerce an unwilling population to accept sudden and painful changes.

At this point, however, the paradox begins. For in order to effect rapid changes, any such centralized regime must mount a vigorous attack on the family lest the traditions of present generations be preserved. It is necessary, in other words, artificially to create an experiential chasm between parents and children to insulate the latter in order that they can more easily be indoctrinated with new ideas. The desire may be to cause an even more total submission to the state, but if one wishes to mold children in order to achieve some future goal, one must begin to view them as superior, inasmuch as they are closer to this future goal. One must also study their needs with care in order to achieve this difficult preparation for the future. One must teach them not to respect their tradition-bound elders, who are tied to the past and know only what is irrelevant. In other words, one must become child-centered and democratic in one's familial policies.[42]

Thus far I have emphasized the causes more than the consequences of the democratic family system. We know that family and state tend to conform to each other in their authority patterns, and each seems to have the capacity to affect the other. As David and Vera Mace point out, "If the state and the family differ fundamentally in the principles and ideals that motivate them, one will ultimately destroy the influence and power of the other."[43] Changes in the state are somewhat more visible, but we have now seen how changes in the family can occur independent of political changes, and once this has taken place it is easy to see how political authoritarianism could be undermined. It is in the family, after all, that attitudes of submissiveness or independence are learned. For the very small child, parents represent the entire universe, and one cannot build an automatic political submissiveness on a foundation of familial independence. This is the paradox: one cannot teach the child to reject parental authority and be able to count on political authoritarianism, but one cannot permit submission to parental authority if one wishes to bring about profound social change.

The consequences of family democratization take a long time to make themselves felt. But even were policy makers to decide that the benefits of rapid social change did not justify these dangerous consequences, it would be difficult to reverse the process once begun. What political intervention in the family initiates, technological change will carry forward. Technological advancement is a primary goal of those nations who are attempting to manipulate family relationships, and once the machinery of technological growth is set in motion, it will drive its own wedges into the family. Whichever force is most responsible, we seem to be witnessing the emergence of increasingly strong pressures toward democratization in the Soviet Union, and although they have been successfully parried or diverted for the most part, they appear to be in the ascendant.

The dangers to an authoritarian regime that follow intervention in the parent-child relationship have not escaped the attention of policy makers, but they have been unable to resolve the dilemma.

Nazi Germany, the Soviet Union, and China have all shown great ambivalence in their approach to the family. The primary Nazi emphasis, as Lewis Coser observes, was on *strengthening* the authoritarian family, but the requirements of totalitarian control and the desire to monopolize individual loyalties forced a degree of competitive intervention. "Nazi policies for family and youth attempted to strengthen the paternalistic family and at the same time attacked and weakened it."[44] How much the familial democratization observed in postwar Germany can be attributed to this intervention is uncertain, since there have been other powerful forces for change.

For the Soviet Union and China the balance is tipped the other way. Both revolutionary regimes began with a frontal attack on the traditional family, only to draw back as they became aware of the consequences. "The Russian policy-makers now realize that the authoritarian family acts as a 'transmission belt' for the inculcation of the authoritarian norms of the total society. They apparently feel that this task was not sufficiently well performed by the extrafamilial institutions for socialization."[45] But for the first fifteen or twenty years after the revolution the assault on the traditional bourgeois patriarchal family was intense. We find Soviet leaders in the early period clearly supporting youth in opposition to a "reactionary" older generation. Actual public denunciation of parents by children was probably rare, as the Maces point out. But "parents tended to suppress their disagreement with the political opinions of their children, and to make the best of the situation. The evidence further suggests that Soviet parents, like most others, are eager for their children to make a success of life," which necessitated sustaining their loyalty to the regime.[46] In other words, once the wedge is driven it makes very little difference how one tries to manipulate it. *Once uncertainty is created in the parent how best to prepare the child for the future—once the parent can in any way imagine his own orientation to be a possible liability to the child in the world approaching—the authoritarian family is moribund,* regardless of whatever countermeasures may be taken. Indeed, it is likely that attempts to undo the process, such as the highly conservative Soviet family policies of the 1930s and 1940s, only serve to aggravate it. "The state, by its very interference in the life of its citizens, must necessarily undermine a parental authority which it attempts to restore."[47] Official denials that there is any conflict of interest between family and state, official exhortations to respect parents "even if they are old-fashioned" (with support like this parental authority surely needs no opposition) can hardly serve to restore parental confidence that their way is the only way.[48]

Such self-doubt seems only right and proper to us, for we have been accustomed for centuries to the notion that the future will be different from the present (and we hope better) and that what was good for the parents may not be good for the children. In the Soviet Union, however, the traditional family is still a live issue, as was illustrated in a movie released a few years ago in this country under the title *A Summer to Remember*. It concerns some events in the life of a small boy, and its implicit child-rearing prescriptions seem quite American. The child's mother, however, represents the old school, and in one scene punishes the child for calling his uncle (who has teased him rather sadistically) a fool. The somewhat idealized step-father, who is permissive and affectionate toward the child, rejects his wife's view that adults should always be respected, and protests that the boy should not be punished for speaking the truth. The film ends with the stepfather deciding at the very last minute to reverse an earlier decision and take the child, who has been ill, to a desolate frontier town in Siberia. The child's joy at being included involves some irony, since he has endowed what the parents know to be an almost intolerable habitation with all the glamor that a child can attach to the unknown and unattainable. Thus it is a situation in which the parents, after all, *do* know more than the child. One can imagine them remonstrating with him, following his first disillusioned complaint about their new home: "But you *begged* us to bring you, and we *told* you how it would be." Yet, *do* they know more? Would a milder climate outweigh the parents' presence as a factor in the child's recovery? And will the child really hate Siberia as they do, or will he perhaps feel more comfortable in it? After all, he does not have their prejudices and preferences. How is one to know? Since the future belongs to him, perhaps his wishes are the safest chance.

China appears to have undergone a similar cycle. The old patriarchal family was, of course, in retreat long before the Communists came to power, but it was they who mounted the total attack that seems finally to have routed it. Yet only a decade after the defeat of the Kuomintang army, signs of second thoughts about the attack on parental power began to appear. The slogan "all for the children" was surrounded with qualifications, and the positive side of filial piety received some attention. As Goode observes, these second thoughts "do not herald a return to the traditional family. They represent no more than official recognition that the propaganda campaign against the power of the elders may lead to misunderstanding on the part of the young, who may at times abandon their filial responsibilities to the state."[49]

The case of the kibbutz is also of interest in this connection, for here there is no issue of protecting the power base of the state, and hence the attack on the traditional family has been wholehearted and unhesitating. Like the Puritans, the kibbutz founders sought to establish an ideal community in the wilderness, uncontaminated by the viciousness of existing institutions, but unlike the earlier group they viewed the authoritarian family as the foundation stone not of the new community but of existing corruption, and attempted to eradicate it altogether.

Now it could be argued that the attack on the traditional family undermines authoritarian submission to the state only because the latter is not vigorous enough in usurping the parental role. If the state should make itself the parent, then the transmission belt function of the family would become unnecessary. But with many of the kibbutzim this deficiency has been largely rectified, and although their position and goals differ markedly from those of the major Communist states, it will be interesting to see how collective child-rearing affects attitudes toward the community.

From studies already carried out it seems apparent that a generalized affection and loyalty to the kibbutz has been achieved—there has been no mass exodus of the sabras (individuals born in Israel). On the other hand, there have been widespread complaints that the sabras hold certain collective sentiments less dear than did the kibbutz founders. They are more concerned with privacy and tend to be more family-centered.[50] As we might have expected, the sabras, being more comfortable in and better adapted to the new life than their parents, feel somewhat superior to them, and regard them as rather old-fashioned and bourgeois. By the same token they appear to have rejected Judaism and to have evolved a highly negative stereotype of Jewishness.[51] But in this they are after all only expressing the orientation of their parents in somewhat extreme form. A more significant outcome is the tendency of the sabras to be apolitical and anti-ideological. Although loyal to the kibbutz and admiring of the Soviet Union, they seem generally bored with Marxism and perfunctory in their commitment to Marxist ideals. Melford Spiro makes the following point about this tendency:

"The Party, through which [political] activity is expressed, demands strict party discipline—which means acceptance of its authority. But the sabras have little respect for authority; obedience to authority is of little importance in their value system."[52]

One of the interesting sidelights of Spiro's study of the sabras is that many of their characteristics recall descriptions of our own population: pragmatism, indifference to ideology, fear of isolation from the group, love of bigness, status-consciousness, and so on. This is not altogether surprising, despite the profound differences in ideology and child-rearing arrangements, since in many respects the kibbutz is simply suburbia carried to its logical extreme. Both derive from an anti-urban nostalgia and a desire to form a homogeneous community of like-minded individuals. Our country, it is important to remember, was founded, built, populated, and sustained by individuals whose characteristic response to social problems was flight, escape, and avoidance.[53] The suburb also springs from this impulse. But there are also similarities in the attitudes toward child-rearing: child-centeredness, permissiveness, an attempt to eliminate the authority issue from the parent-child relationship and be pals, and a willingness to sacrifice current living standards in order that the children may live better, with the result that reaching adulthood involves some material deprivation. Furthermore, the newer suburbs often place the child in a narrow age-graded environment, leading to a strong emphasis on peer groups and a diminished sense of the total range of ages in the society. While still far removed from the kibbutz nursery, our society has consistently moved toward a lower and lower age of both formal and informal peer contact. Calhoun remarked a half-century ago that "the kindergarten grows downward toward the cradle and there arises talk of neighborhood nurseries,"[54] a trend that has accelerated in recent years, along with more informal arrangements for peer group contact among preschool children.

The comparison should not be overdrawn, of course, but what I am trying to emphasize is that an orientation toward the future tends to generate certain common attributes, regardless of differences in ideology and intent. At the present moment it seems clear that the entire globe is being swiftly drawn into such an orientation from a wide variety of positions and perspectives, and if my reasoning is correct, it follows with some inevitability that the democratic family and ultimately the mass democratic state, in some form or another, will become universal. This is not an event likely to trouble or please any living person, to be sure, and there are many more pressing issues alive in the world today, some of which could make this prediction not only incorrect but irrelevant. Nor does this single area of convergence necessarily betoken a disappearance of the rich variety of social arrangements which has been so essential to the evolution of human culture. But it does suggest that at least some of the troublesome issues of our own society may become universal by the time another century has passed, assuming that civilization and indeed human life still obtain on this planet. At such a time alternative visions will be far more difficult to imagine. Our society has lived with the joys and miseries of the democratic family longer than any other, and it is here that its problems could most profitably be examined. The characteristic American approach to social problems—chronic denial interspersed with occasional brief flurries of murderous punitiveness—is a prohibitive luxury in the complex and tiny world we inhabit today; and the burden of confrontation is often lightened by anticipation.

3

Beyond Bureaucracy

———⊙———

Change continues to be the one given of our time—dizzying, unpredictable, relentless change that all but cries out for temporary systems that can be dismantled as soon as they become outmoded. Ask those who have the unenviable task of keeping the map of the world up to date. As new nations spring up almost weekly, those harried cartographers must wish they were working on an Etch-a-Sketch.

The organizations that thrive today are those that embrace change instead of trying to resist it. The old Weberian bureaucracies are simply too slow, too weighed down with intraorganizational agendas and priorities, to compete in a world where success goes to those who can identify and solve problems almost before they have names. Thirty years ago, I thought rigid, pyramidal organizations were doomed largely for theoretical reasons. Now I see they are doomed because they simply do not work or, more precisely, because they do not work fast enough. Today's most viable institutions are dancers, not marchers. They see opportunities, exploit them, and then move nimbly onto the next challenge, while the heavy bureaucratic bears are still gearing up to study the problem at hand.

One chapter of the book deserves special mention: Chapter One, "Democracy Is Inevitable." When Phil Slater and I first wrote that essay and submitted it to the *Harvard Business Review*, a cautious editor there insisted that we hedge our bets and requested that we change the title to "Is Democracy Inevitable?" Even ten years ago, the editor's caution seemed prudent. The Cold War had thawed little since the big chill of the 1950s. Then, only a few years ago, the barely imaginable happened. First, the Berlin Wall tumbled. Then, the Soviet Union, that heaviest of bureaucratic bears, fell apart like a bad marriage. Suddenly, Phil and I looked like the academic princes of prescience. In 1990, the *Harvard Business Review* reissued the essay as a classic. I don't know about you, but I get up every morning and thank God for the dissolution of the Soviet Union. The take-home lessons? Timing is all.

In the course of my crystal-gazing thirty-five years ago, I missed several things. My confidence that the United States would become an "educated society" is weaker now than it was then. Deepening poverty, government neglect, and other factors have reduced American standardized test scores to new lows. Public schools, at least those in large cities, are a national scandal.

In its emphasis on the growing importance of organizational interdependence, I suggested that globalization will grow in the future. Now that the future is here, it is clear that I underestimated the importance of globalization as an organizational trend. Global corporations have become the very models of postbureaucratic organization, able to orchestrate a worldwide network of component units skilled at exploiting the specific realities of their local communities. In the 1960s, we spoke confidently of the emergence of a global village, but few of us truly appreciated how new technologies, particularly those that make instant communication possible, would all but erase national borders.

Like virtually every other prognosticator of my generation, I failed to predict the critical role Japan would play in organizational life of the post–1960s. Japan's contribution to management theory and practice in recent years has constituted a virtual paradigm shift. I predict the rest of the Pacific Rim will have as important an influence on world business in the 1990s and beyond.

Finally, I wish I had been able then—or were able now—to come up with a better term for the temporary systems I had so much faith in. To this day, no deathless term comes to mind. *Adaptive systems* or *organic systems* is probably better than *temporary systems*, but not much. Some people like the term *learning systems*, but that, too, is insufficiently pungent. We still need to find a phrase that captures the ability of temporary systems to stay viable by continually transforming themselves to meet the demands of changing climates.

One of the surprises of rereading this essay was the discovery that it is essentially an outline of my intellectual preoccupations of the last few decades. I continue to be fascinated by the tension in organizations between personal actualization—freedom, if you will—and the achievement of institutional goals. I continue to have faith in science, with its respect for dissent and its commitment to experimentation, as a model for organizational viability. And I am more interested than ever in creative collaboration, the process whereby a group pools its talents and creates something that transcends the contribution of the individuals.

My interest in how change is accomplished, which permeates this essay and the entire book, led almost inevitably to my subsequent studies of leadership. The autocratic man (and he was always a man) whose organization was his lengthened shadow is dead. The leaders of yesteryear were preoccupied with three objectives: control, order, and predictability. The postbureaucratic organization requires a new kind of leader: one who can inspire and empower.

Tomorrow's organizations will be federations, networks, clusters, cross-functional teams, temporary systems, ad hoc task forces, lattices, modules, matrices—almost anything but pyramids. The successful ones will make problem finding, not problem solving, their first priority. They will be led by people who embrace error, even the occasional failure, because they know it will teach them more than success. Such organizations will be led by people who understand, as scientists do, the primal pleasure of the hunt that is problem solving.

In the postbureaucratic world, the laurel will go to the leader who encourages healthy dissent and values those followers courageous enough to say no. It will go to the leader who exults in cultural differences and knows that diversity is the best hope for long-term survival. These new leaders will not have the loudest voice, but the

most attentive ear. Instead of pyramids, these postbureaucratic organizations will be structures built of energy and ideas, led by people
who find their joy in the task at hand, not in leaving monuments
behind.

———◦◉◦———

Not far from the new government center in downtown Boston, a
foreign visitor walked up to a sailor and asked why American ships
were built to last only a short time. According to the tourist, "The
sailor answered without hesitation that the art of navigation is making such rapid progress that the finest ship would become obsolete if
it lasted beyond a few years. In these words which fell accidentally
from an uneducated man, I began to recognize the general and systematic idea upon which your great people direct all their concerns."[1]

The foreign visitor was that shrewd observer of American morals
and manners, Alexis de Tocqueville, and the year was 1835. He
would not recognize Scollay Square today. But he had caught the
central theme of our country: its preoccupation, its obsession with
change. One thing is new, however, since de Tocqueville's time: the
acceleration of newness, the changing scale and scope of change
itself as Dr. Robert Oppenheimer said, " . . . the world alters as we
walk in it, so that the years of man's life measure not some small
growth or rearrangement or moderation of what was learned in
childhood, but a great upheaval."[2]

In the previous chapter, we discussed the impact of these changes
on the American family. Let us now turn to an examination of how
these accelerating changes in our society will influence other human
organizations.

In Chapter One, we predicted the end of bureaucracy as we
know it and the rise of new social systems better suited to the twentieth-century demands of industrialization. This forecast was based
on the evolutionary principle that every age develops an organizational form appropriate to its genius, and that the prevailing form,
known by sociologists as bureaucracy and by many businessmen as
"damn bureaucracy," is out of joint with contemporary realities.

I should like to make clear that by bureaucracy I mean a chain of command structured on the lines of a pyramid—the typical structure that coordinates the business of almost every human organization we know of: industrial, governmental, educational, investigatory, military, religious, and voluntary. I do not have in mind those fantasies so often dreamed up to describe complex organizations. These fantasies can be summarized in two grotesque stereotypes. The first I call "organization as ink blot"—an actor steals around an uncharted wasteland, growing more restive and paranoid by the hour, while he awaits orders that never come. The other specter is "organization as big daddy"—the actors are square people plugged into square holes by some omniscient and omnipotent genius who can cradle in his arms the destiny of man by way of computer and TV. Whatever the first image owes to Kafka, the second owes to George Orwell's *1984*.

Bureaucracy, as I refer to it here, is a useful social invention that was perfected during the industrial revolution to organize and direct the activities of a business firm. Most students of organizations would say that its anatomy consists of the following components:

A well-defined chain of command

A system of procedures and rules for dealing with all contingencies relating to work activities

A division of labor based on specialization

Promotion and selection based on technical competence

Impersonality in human relations

It is the pyramid arrangement we see on most organizational charts.

The bureaucratic "machine model" was developed as a reaction against the personal subjugation, nepotism, cruelty, and the capricious and subjective judgments that passed for managerial practices during the early days of the industrial revolution. Bureaucracy emerged out of the organizations' need for order and precision and the workers' demands for impartial treatment. It was an organization ideally suited to the values and demands of the Victorian era. And just as bureaucracy emerged as a creative response to a radically new age, so today new organizational shapes are surfacing before our eyes.

First I shall try to show why the conditions of our modern industrialized world will bring about the death of bureaucracy. In the second part of this chapter I will suggest a rough model of the organization of the future.

There are at least four relevant threats to bureaucracy:

1. Rapid and unexpected change
2. Growth in size where the volume of an organization's traditional activities is not enough to sustain growth (A number of factors are included here, among them: bureaucratic overhead; tighter controls and impersonality due to bureaucratic sprawls; outmoded rules and organizational structures.)
3. Complexity of modern technology where integration between activities and persons of very diverse, highly specialized competence is required
4. A basically psychological threat springing from a change in managerial behavior

It might be useful to examine the extent to which these conditions exist right now.

Rapid and Unexpected Change

Bureaucracy's strength is its capacity to manage efficiently the routine and predictable in human affairs. It is almost enough to cite the knowledge and population explosion to raise doubts about its contemporary viability. More revealing, however, are the statistics that demonstrate these overworked phrases:

> Our productivity output per man hour may now be doubling almost every twenty years rather than every forty years, as it did before World War II.

The federal government alone spent 16 billion dollars in research and development activities in 1965; it will spend 35 billion dollars by 1980.

The time lag between a technical discovery and recognition of its commercial uses was thirty years before World War I, sixteen years between the wars, and only nine years since World War II.

In 1946, only forty-two cities in the world had populations of more than one million. Today there are ninety. In 1930, there were forty people for each square mile of the earth's land surface. Today [1968] there are sixty-three. By 2000, it is expected, the figure will have soared to 142.

Bureaucracy with its nicely defined chain of command, its rules, and its rigidities is ill-adapted to the rapid change the environment now demands.

Growth in Size

While, in theory, there may be no natural limit to the height of a bureaucratic pyramid, in practice the element of complexity is almost invariably introduced with great size. International operation, to cite one significant new element, is the rule rather than exception for most of our biggest corporations. Firms like Standard Oil Company (New Jersey) with more than one hundred foreign affiliates, Mobil Oil Corporation, The National Cash Register Company, Singer Company, Burroughs Corporation, and Colgate-Palmolive Company derive more than half their income or earnings from foreign sales. Many others—such as Eastman Kodak Company, Chas. Pfizer & Company, Inc., Caterpillar Tractor Company, International Harvester Company, Corn Products Company, and Minnesota Mining & Manufacturing Company—make from 30 to 50 percent of their sales abroad. General Motors Corporation sales are not only nine times those of Volkswagen, they are also bigger than the gross national product of the Netherlands and well over the GNP of a hundred other countries. If we have seen the sun set on the British Empire, we may never see it set on the empires of General Motors, ITT, Shell, and Unilever.[3]

Increasing Diversity

Today's activities require persons of very diverse, highly specialized competence.

Numerous dramatic examples can be drawn from studies of labor markets and job mobility. At some point during the past decade, the United States became the first nation ever to employ more people in service occupations than in the production of tangible goods. Examples of this trend follow:

> In the field of education, the *increase* in employment between 1950 and 1960 was greater than the total number employed in the steel, copper, and aluminum industries.

> In the field of health, the *increase* in employment between 1950 and 1960 was greater than the total employment in mining in 1960.

These changes, plus many more that are harder to demonstrate statistically, break down the old, industrial trend toward more and more people doing either simple or undifferentiated chores.

Hurried growth, rapid change, and increase in specialization—pit these three factors against the five components of the pyramid structure described earlier, and we should expect the pyramid of bureaucracy to begin crumbling.

Change in Managerial Behavior

There is, I believe, a subtle but perceptible change in the philosophy underlying management behavior. Its magnitude, nature, and antecedents, however, are shadowy because of the difficulty of assigning numbers. (Whatever else statistics do for us, they provide a welcome illusion of certainty.) Nevertheless, real change seems under way because of

A new concept of *man* based on increased knowledge of his complex and shifting needs, which replaces an oversimplified, innocent, push-button idea of man

A new concept of *power*, based on collaboration and reason, which replaces a model of power based on coercion and threat

A new concept of *organizational values*, based on humanistic-democratic ideals, which replaces the depersonalized, mechanistic value system of bureaucracy

The primary cause of this shift in management philosophy stems not from the bookshelf but from managers themselves. Many of the behavioral scientists, like Douglas McGregor or Rensis Likert, have clarified and articulated—even legitimized—what managers have only half registered to themselves. I am convinced, for example, that the popularity of McGregor's book, *The Human Side of Enterprise*, was based on his rare empathy for a vast audience of managers who are wistful for an alternative to the mechanistic concept of authority, that is, he outlined a vivid utopia of more authentic human relationships than most organizational practices today allow. Furthermore, I suspect that the desire for relationships in business has little to do with a profit motive per se, though it is often rationalized as doing so. The real push for these changes stems from the need, not only to humanize the organization but to use it as a crucible of personal growth and the development of self-realization.[4]

Another aspect of this shift in values has to do with man's historical quest for self-awareness, for using reason to achieve and stretch his potentialities, his possibilities. This deliberate self-analysis has spread to large and more complex social systems—organizations, where there has been a dramatic upsurge of this spirit of inquiry over the past two decades. At new depths and over a wider range of affairs, organizations are opening their operations to self-inquiry and self-analysis, which involves a change in how the men who make history and the men who make knowledge regard each other. The scientists have realized their affinity with men of affairs, and the latter have found a new receptivity and respect for men of knowledge.

I am calling this new development "organizational revitalization," a complex social process that involves a deliberate and self-conscious examination of organizational behavior and a collaborative relationship between managers and scientists to improve performance. For many this new form of collaboration can be taken for granted. I have simply regarded reciprocity between the academician and manager as inevitable and natural. But I can assure you that this development is unprecedented, that never before in history, in any society, has man in his organizational context so willingly searched, scrutinized, examined, inspected, or contemplated—for meaning, for purpose, for improvement.

This shift in outlook has taken a good deal of courage from both partners in this encounter. The manager has had to shake off old prejudices about "eggheads" and "long-hair" intellectuals. More important, the manager has had to make himself and his organization vulnerable and receptive to external sources and to new, unexpected, even unwanted information. The academician has had to shed some of his natural hesitancies. Scholarly conservatism is admirable except as something to hide behind, and for a long time caution was a defense against reality.

It might be useful to dwell a bit longer on the role of academic man and his growing involvement with social action, using the field of management education as a case in point. Until recently, the field of business was unknown to, or snubbed by, the academic establishment. There, management education and research were at best regarded with dark suspicion as if contact with the world of reality—particularly monetary reality—was equivalent to a dreadful form of pollution.

In fact, historically, academic man has taken one of two stances toward "the establishment," any establishment: that of a rebellious critic or of a withdrawn snob. The stance of the rebel can be seen in such paperback titles as *The Power Elite*, *The Lonely Crowd*, *Organization Man*, *The Hidden Persuaders*, *Tyranny of Testing*, *Mass Leisure*, *Growing Up Absurd*, *The Paper Economy*, *Silent Spring*, *The Affluent Society*, and *Depleted Society*.

The withdrawn stance can still be observed in some of our American universities, but less so these days. However, it continues to be the prevailing attitude in many European universities. There the universities seem intent on preserving the monastic ethos of their medieval origins, offering a lulling security to their inmates, and sapping the curriculum of virility and relevance. Max Beerbohm's whimsical and idyllic fantasy of Oxford, *Zuleika Dobson*, dramatizes this:

> It is the mild, miasmal air, not less than the grey beauty and the gravity of the buildings that has helped Oxford to produce and foster, externally, her peculiar race of artist-scholars, scholar-artists. . . . The Buildings and their traditions keep astir in his mind whatsoever is gracious; the climate enfolding and enfeebling him, lulling him, keeps him careless of the sharp, harsh exigent realities of the outerworld. These realities may be seen by him. . . . But they cannot fire him. Oxford is too damp for that.[5]

"Adorable Dreamer," said Matthew Arnold, in his valedictory to Oxford:

> Adorable dreamer, whose heart has been so romantic! who has given thyself so prodigally, given thyself to sides and to heroes not mine, only never to the Philistine! . . . what teacher could ever so save us from that bondage to which we are all prone . . . the bondage of what binds us all, the narrow, the mundane, the merely practical.

The intellectual and the manager have only recently come out of hiding and recognized the enormous possibilities of joint ventures. Remember that the idea of the professional school is new, even in the case of the venerable threesome—law, medicine, and engineering—to say nothing of recent upstarts like business and public administration. It is as new as the institutionalization of science itself, say around fifty years. And even today, this change is not greeted with unmixed joy. Colin Clark, the economist, writing in a recent issue of the magazine *Encounter*, referred to the "dreadful suggestion that Oxford ought to have a business school."[6]

It is probably true that in the United States we have had a more pragmatic attitude toward knowledge than anywhere else. Many observers have been impressed with the disdain European intellectuals seem to show for practical matters. Even in Russia, where one would least expect it, there is little interest in the "merely useful." Harrison Salisbury, of the *New York Times*, was struck during his travels in the Soviet Union by the almost total absence of liaison between research and practical application. He saw only one agricultural experiment station on the American model. There, professors were working in the fields and told him, "People call us Americans."

There may not be many American professors working in the fields, but they can be found, when not waiting in airports, almost everywhere else: in factories, in government, in less-advanced countries, and more recently, in backward areas of our own country, in mental hospitals, in the State Department, in practically all the institutional crevices Ph.D. candidates can worm their way into. They are advising, counseling, researching, recruiting, interpreting, developing, consulting, training, and working for the widest variety of clients imaginable. This is not to say that the deep ambivalence some Americans hold toward the intellectual has disappeared, but it does indicate that academic man has become more committed to action, in greater numbers, with more diligence, and with higher aspirations than at any other time in history.

Indeed, Fritz Machlup, the economist, has coined a new economic category called the "knowledge industry," which, he claims, accounts for 29 percent of the gross national product. And Clark Kerr, the former president of the University of California, said not too long ago

> What the railroads did for the second half of the last century and the automobile did for the first half of this century may be done for the second half of this century by the knowledge industry: that is, to serve as the focal point of national growth. And the university is at the center of the knowledge process.[7]

The core problems confronting any organization can be categorized into six major areas. First, let us consider the problems (see Table 3.1), then let us see how our twentieth-century conditions of constant change have made the bureaucratic approach to these problems obsolete. We start with the problem of how man's needs can be fused with the needs and goals of his employing organization.

Integration

The problem is how to integrate individual needs and organizational goals. In other words, it is the inescapable conflict between individual needs (like spending time with the family) and organizational demands (like meeting deadlines).

Under twentieth-century conditions of constant change there has been an emergence of human sciences and a deeper understanding of man's complexity. Today, integration encompasses the entire range of issues concerned with incentives, rewards, and motivations of the individual and how the organization succeeds or fails in adjusting to these issues. In our society, where personal attachments play an important role, the individual is appreciated, and there is genuine concern for his well-being, not just in a veterinary-hygiene sense, but as a moral, integrated personality.

Table 3.1. Human Problems Confronting Contemporary Organizations.

Problem	Bureaucratic Solutions	New Twentieth-Century Conditions
Integration		
Integrating individual needs and organizational goals.	No solution because there is no problem. Individual vastly oversimplified, regarded as passive instrument. Tension between personality and role disregarded.	Emergence of human sciences and understanding of man's complexity. Rising aspirations. Humanistic-democratic ethos.
Social Influence		
Distributing power and sources of power and authority.	An explicit reliance on legal-rational power, but an implicit usage of coercive power. In any case, a confused, ambiguous, shifting complex of competence, coercion, and legal code.	Separation of management from ownership. Rise of trade unions and general education. Negative and unintended effects of authoritarian rule.
Collaboration		
Producing mechanisms for the control of conflict.	The "rule of hierarchy" to resolve conflicts between ranks and the "rule of coordination" to resolve conflict between horizontal groups. Loyalty.	Specialization and professionalization and increased need for interdependence. Leadership too complex for one-man rule or omniscience.

Adaptation Responding appropriately to changes induced by the environment.		External environment of firm more turbulent, less predictable. Unprecedented rate of technological change.
Identity Achieving clarity, consensus, and commitment to organizational goals.		Increased complexity due to diversity, multipurpose capability, intersector mobility. Creates role complexity, conflict, and ambiguity.
Revitalization Dealing with growth and decay.	Underlying assumption that the future will be certain and at least basically similar to the past.	Rapid changes in technologies, tasks, manpower, raw materials, norms and values of society, goals of enterprise and society all make constant attention to the process of revision imperative.

Paradoxical Twins

The problem of integration, like most human problems, has a venerable past. The modern version goes back at least 160 years and was precipitated by a historical paradox: the twin births of modern individualism and modern industrialism. The former brought about a deep concern for and a passionate interest in the individual and his personal rights. The latter brought about increased mechanization of organized activity. Competition between the two has intensified as each decade promises more freedom and hope for man and more stunning achievements for technology. I believe that our society *has* opted for more humanistic and democratic values, however unfulfilled they may be in practice. It will "buy" these values even at loss in efficiency because it feels it can now afford the loss.

Social Influence

This problem is essentially one of power and of how power is distributed. It is a complex issue and alive with controversy, partly because of an ethical component and partly because studies of leadership and power distribution can be interpreted in many ways, and almost always in ways that coincide with one's biases (including a cultural leaning toward democracy).

The problem of power has to be seriously reconsidered because of dramatic situational changes that make the possibility of one-man rule not necessarily "bad," but impractical. I refer to changes in top management's role.

Peter Drucker listed forty-one major responsibilities of the chief executive and declared that "90 percent of the trouble we are having with the chief executive's job is rooted in our superstition of the one-man chief."[8] Many factors make one-man control obsolete, among them the broadening product base of industry; the impact of new technology; the scope of international operation; the separation of management from ownership; the rise of trade unions; and the dissemination of general education. The real power of the chief has been eroding in most organizations even though both he and the organization cling to the older concept.

Collaboration

This is the problem of managing and resolving conflicts. Bureaucratically, it grows out of the very same social process of conflict and stereotyping that has divided nations and communities. As organizations become more complex, they fragment and divide, building tribal patterns and symbolic codes, which often work to exclude others (secrets and jargon, for example) and on occasion to exploit differences for inward (and always fragile) harmony.

Recent research is shedding new light on the problem of conflict. Psychologist Robert R. Blake in his stunning experiments has shown how simple it is to induce conflict, how difficult to arrest it. He takes two groups of people who have never before been together, gives them a task that will be judged by an impartial jury. In less than an hour, each group devolves into a tightly knit band with all the symptoms of an "in" group. They regard their product as a "masterwork" and the other group's as commonplace at best. "Other" becomes "enemy." "We are good, they are bad; we are right, they are wrong."[9]

Jaap Rabbie, conducting experiments on intergroup conflict at the University of Utrecht, has been amazed by the ease with which conflict and stereotype develop. He brings into an experimental room two groups and distributes green name tags and pens to one group, red pens and tags to the other. The two groups do not compete; they do not even interact. They are only in sight of each other while they silently complete a questionnaire. Only ten minutes are needed to activate defensiveness and fear, reflected in the hostile and irrational perceptions of both "reds" and "greens."[10]

In a recent essay on animal behavior, Harvard professor Erik Erikson develops the idea of "pseudo-species." Pseudo-species act as if they were separate species created at the beginning of time by supernatural intent. He argues

> Man has evolved (by whatever kind of evolution and for whatever adaptive reasons) in pseudo-species, e.g., tribes, clans, classes, etc. Thus, each develops not only a distinct sense of identity but also a conviction of harboring *the* human identity, fortified against other pseudo-species by prejudices which mark them as extra specific and inimical to "genuine" human endeavor. Paradoxically, however, newly born man is (to use Ernst Mayr's term) a generalist creature who could be made to fit into any number of pseudo-species and must, therefore, become "specialized during a prolonged childhood."[11]

Modern organizations abound with pseudo-species, bands of specialists held together by the illusion of a unique identity and with a tendency to view other pseudo-species with suspicion and mistrust.

Adaptation

The real *coup de grâce* to bureaucracy has come as much from the turbulent environment as from its incorrect assumptions about human behavior. The pyramidal structure of bureaucracy, where power was concentrated at the top—perhaps by one person who had the knowledge and resources to control the entire enterprise—seemed perfect to run a railroad. And undoubtedly, for tasks like building railroads, for the routinized tasks of the nineteenth and early twentieth centuries, bureaucratic centuries, bureaucracy was and is an eminently suitable social arrangement.

Today, due primarily to the growth of science, technology, and research and development activities, the organizational environment of organizations is rapidly changing. It is a turbulent environment, not a placid and predictable one, and there is a deepening interdependence among the economic and other facets of society. This means the economic organizations are increasingly enmeshed in legislation and public policy. Put more simply, it means that the government will be more involved, more of the time. It may also mean, and this is radical, that maximizing cooperation rather than competition between organizations—particularly if their fates are correlated (which is most certainly to be common)—may become a strong possibility.

Identity

Organizations never refer to it as such, but they are as allergic to identity crises as adolescents. College students seem to recover from theirs shortly after graduation, whereas organizations are never fully "cured" and may re-experience the anxiety at different phases of organizational development. When an individual is vague, mixed-up, and uncertain about who he is or where he is going, we call it "identity diffusion." An identity crisis can be experienced as well when an individual experiences constriction of choice and possibilities.

In organizations, the problem of identity has many of the same properties as "diffusion" and "constraint," but most often it is discussed in terms of the degree to which the organization is clear about and committed to its goals. Modern organizations are extremely vulnerable to an identity problem for many of the reasons discussed earlier, but chiefly because rapid growth and turbulence transform and distort the original, more simplified goals. An organization, for example, attains riches and fame for an invention and then discovers it is in the business of production without ever truly deciding on that. A university sets out pure and simple to transmit knowledge to students, but suddenly finds that 50 percent of its budget comes from government research grants and finds itself part of the defense industry.

What makes matters worse is the fact that organizational complexity and diversity lead to differing orientations within subsystems so that goals that may be clear and identified within one part of the organization are antithetical, or at best only vaguely understood, by other subsystems of the organization.

Constant surveillance of the primary tasks is a necessity, particularly if the organization is embedded in a dynamic, protean environment.

Revitalization

This is the problem of growth and decay. As Alfred North Whitehead has said: "The art of free society consists first in the maintenance of the symbolic code, and secondly, in the fearlessness of revision. . . . Those societies which cannot combine reverence to their symbols with freedom of revision must ultimately decay. . . ."

Growth and decay emerge as the penultimate conditions of contemporary society. Organizations, as well as societies, must be concerned with those social structures that engender buoyancy, resilience, and a fearlessness of revision.

I introduce the term *revitalization* to embrace all the social mechanisms that stagnate and regenerate, as well as the process of this cycle. The elements of revitalization are

> An ability to learn from experience and to codify, store, and retrieve the relevant knowledge
>
> An ability to learn how to learn, that is, to develop methods for improving the learning process
>
> An ability to acquire and use feedback mechanisms on performance, in short, to be self-analytical
>
> An ability to direct one's own destiny

These qualities have a good deal in common with what John Gardner calls "self-renewal." For the organization, it means conscious attention to its own evolution. Without a planned methodology and explicit direction, the enterprise will not realize its potential.

Integration, distribution of power, collaboration, adaptation, identity, and *revitalization*—these are the major human problems of the next twenty-five years. How organizations cope with and manage these tasks will undoubtedly determine the viability of the enterprise.

Against this background I should like to set forth some of the conditions that will dictate organizational life in the next two or three decades.

The Environment

Rapid technological change and diversification will lead to more and more partnerships between government and business. It will be a truly mixed economy. Because of the immensity and expense of the projects, there will be fewer identical units competing in the same markets and organizations will become more interdependent.

The four main features of this environment are

Interdependence rather than competition

Turbulence and uncertainty rather than readiness and certainty

Large-scale rather than small-scale enterprises

Complex and multinational rather than simple national enterprises

Population Characteristics

The most distinctive characteristic of our society is education. It will become even more so. Within fifteen years, two-thirds of our population living in metropolitan areas will have attended college. Adult education is growing even faster, probably because of the rate of professional obsolescence. The Killian report showed that the average engineer required further education only ten years after getting his degree. It will be almost routine for the experienced physician, engineer, and executive to go back to school for advanced training every two or three years. All of this education is not just "nice." It is necessary.

One other characteristic of the population that will aid our understanding of organizations of the future is increasing job mobility. The ease of transportation, coupled with the needs of a dynamic environment, change drastically the ideas of owning a job or having roots. Already 20 percent of our population change their mailing address at least once a year.

Work Values

The increased level of education and mobility will change the values we place on work. People will be more intellectually committed to their jobs and will probably require more involvement, participation, and autonomy.

Also, people will be more "other-oriented," taking cues for their norms and values from their immediate environment rather than tradition.

Tasks and Goals

The tasks of the organization will be more technical, complicated, and unprogrammed. They will rely on intellect instead of muscle. And they will be too complicated for one person to comprehend, to say nothing of control. Essentially, they will call for the collaboration of specialists in a project or a team form of organization.

There will be a complication of goals. Business will increasingly concern itself with its adaptive or innovative-creative capacity. In addition, supragoals will have to be articulated, goals that shape and provide the foundation for the goal structure. For example, one might be a system for detecting new and changing goals; another could be a system for deciding priorities among goals.

Finally, there will be more conflict and contradiction among diverse standards for organizational effectiveness. This is because professionals tend to identify more with the goals of their profession than with those of their immediate employer. University professors can be used as a case in point. Their inside work may be a conflict between teaching and research, while more of their income is derived from outside sources such as foundations and consultant work. They tend to be poor company men because they divide their loyalty between their professional values and organizational goals.

Organization

The social structure of organizations of the future will have some unique characteristics. The key word will be *temporary*. There will be adaptive, rapidly changing *temporary* systems. These will be task forces organized around problems to be solved by groups of relative strangers with diverse professional skills. The group will be arranged on an organic rather than mechanical model; it will evolve in response to a problem rather than to programmed role expectations. The executive thus becomes coordinator or "linking pin" between various task forces. He must be a man who can speak the polyglot jargon of research, with skills to relay information and to mediate between groups. People will be evaluated not according to rank but according to skill and professional training. Organizational charts will consist of project groups rather than stratified functional groups. (This trend is already visible in the aerospace and construction industries, as well as many professional and consulting firms.)

Adaptive, problem-solving, temporary systems of diverse specialists, linked together by coordinating and task-evaluating executive specialists in an organic flux—this is the organization form that will gradually replace bureaucracy as we know it. As no catchy phrase comes to mind, I call these new-style organizations "*adaptive* structures." Organizational arrangements of this sort may not only reduce the intergroup conflicts mentioned earlier; they may also induce honest-to-goodness creative collaboration.

Motivation

Adaptive organizations should increase motivation and thereby effectiveness, because they create conditions under which the individual can gain increased satisfaction with the task itself. Thus, there should be a harmony between the educated individual's need for tasks that are meaningful, satisfying, and creative *and* an adaptive organizational structure.

Accompanying the increased integration between individual and organizational goals will be new modes of relating and changing commitments to work groups. Most of the research on the individual's relationship to his peer group at work indicates the significance of the work group on performance and morale. The work group creates and reinforces norms and standards, from the appropriate number of units produced to the appropriate amount of interaction and intimacy. The significance of the work group for the communication, control, and regulation of behavior cannot be overestimated. But in the new adaptive organizations I am talking about, work groups will be temporary systems, which means that people will have to learn to develop quick and intense relationships on the job and learn to bear the absence of more enduring work relationships. Thus we should expect to experience a concentration of emotional energy in forming relationships quickly and intensely and then a dissolution and rapid relocation of personal attachments. The following chapter goes into great detail about the social psychological consequences of these emotional acrobatics. From an organizational point of view we can expect that more time and energy will have to be spent on continual rediscovery of the appropriate mix of people, competencies, and tasks within an ambiguous and unstructured existence.

I think that the future I describe is not necessarily a "happy" one. Coping with rapid change, living in temporary work systems, developing meaningful relations and then breaking them—all augur social strains and psychological tensions. Teaching how to live with ambiguity, to identify with the adaptive process, to make a virtue out of contingency, and to be self-directing—these will be the tasks of education, the goals of maturity, and the achievement of the successful individual.

In these new organizations of the future, participants will be called upon to use their minds more than at any other time in history. Fantasy, imagination, and creativity will be legitimate in ways that today seem strange. Social structures will no longer be instruments of psychic repression but will increasingly promote play and freedom on behalf of curiosity and thought.

I started this chapter with a quote from de Tocqueville, and I think it would be fitting to end with one: "I am tempted to believe that what we call necessary institutions are often no more than institutions to which we have grown accustomed. In matters of social constitution, the field of possibilities is much more extensive than men living in their various societies are ready to imagine."[12]

4

Some Social Consequences
of Temporary Systems[1]

=━⟨◉⟩━━

The fear of homogeneity is less marked today than when this book first appeared, but it has by no means vanished. That fear has always been the central feature of 'negative utopias' such as *Brave New World, 1984, Brazil, The Handmaid's Tale*, and a host of sci-fi books and movies. What is terrifying about these fantasies is not so much that everyone is the same but that everyone is the same in some limited and constricting way. Someone's notion of what is right is imposed on everyone else—no one is allowed to be fully human.

This last sentence, however, could be a definition of culture. There is not, nor has there ever been, a society to which it did not apply to some extent. The terror of negative utopias is merely that they are extreme—the rules are very limiting and are rigidly and punitively applied.

All societies make demands for conformity, but the demands we notice, and may therefore resist, are rarely as important as those we adhere to without thinking. We tend to be aware of norms whose violation brings punishment, but in creating conformity the carrot is far more effective than the stick. "That's a good soldier" is much more coercive in the long run than "Don't cry," and no laws are needed to ensure that Americans will adhere to individualistic values. We all know what kinds of nonconformity we've been punished for, but we are far less aware of the kinds of conformity we have been rewarded for. Often the rewards are tacit, and even those doing the rewarding may not be able to verbalize what they are rewarding or

why. We cannot begin to know all the ways we have been programmed to behave—so much is automatic and unconscious. This
is why negative utopias are so fascinating to us. We don't quite know
how we got to be the way we are, and we think we ought to know.

Cults fascinate us for the same reason. Most try to impose a narrow range of behavior on their followers, making them as homogeneous as possible on this limited model. This is why cults tend to be
short-lived. No group can survive for long without access to the full
range of human behavior. As noted below, "a viable society must
somehow avail itself of a great variety of contradictory human
responses." If it limits its repertory too much it will die.

All during the late 1950s and early 1960s Americans were obsessed with the fear that we were all becoming alike—that in the
future every American would be a gray-flannel-suited robot being
driven to the commuter train in a station wagon by a June Cleaver
clone. Instead, there was a cultural explosion—the civil rights movement, the Vietnam War protests, the hippie movement, the sexual
revolution, the women's movement, leading to the complex multi-
cultural society we live in today. The change is reflected on TV. In
place of the bland, lily-white, traditional, suburban, heavily cen-
sored, and largely interchangeable family sitcoms of the 1950s, we
now have a rich variety of social situations and personal arrangements on view, and although no one would claim it to be represen-
tative (some groups are still virtually ignored on the networks), not
even the most confirmed crank would argue that TV is homogeneous, especially in comparison with the shows of thirty years ago.

People back then also did considerable hand-wringing over the
spread of American food products around the globe: the "Coca-
colonization" of the third world and the appearance of McDonald's
in every country. All the great cuisines of the world would be lost,
they complained, as our own worst eating habits spread everywhere.
Once again people assumed that the forms of one specialized group
would be imposed on everyone else. But now it is thirty years later,
and although McDonald's and Coca-Cola have indeed spread all
over the world, foreign cuisines have in equal measure spread all over
the United States. Every major city in the nation, and a great many

minor ones, can boast of Chinese, Japanese, Thai, Vietnamese, Italian, French, German, Mexican, Cuban, African, and other ethnic restaurants. The fear that wherever you go it will be the same is considerably diluted when "the same" includes all possibilities.

The first edition argued that in a highly mobile and temporary society the degree of hiddenness in interpersonal relations that we have always taken for granted would no longer be viable. Emotional distance would be achieved by transience; for relationships to be satisfying they would have to be more open. One sometimes feels a little impatient today with the great novels and dramas of the past, whose pathos depended so heavily on bad communication—lives destroyed because people were unable to express what they felt at a particular moment. We have to immerse ourselves in the cultural assumptions of the story's time and place in order not to feel the whole thing was rather silly.

Two trends today may further reflect the need for more openness in modern society. One is the radical assault women are making today on the traditional male ineptness at emotional communication. In the past this defect was considered a virtue, and the masculine tradition of stumbling around mutely, weighted down with a crippling load of grim psychological armor, was an unquestioned tenet of the patriarchal status quo. Today it is in retreat as men themselves begin to be less willing to pay the price of emotional strangulation.

A second trend is the prevalence in the media of what might be called foible comedy—the expression and exposure for comic recognition of the most petty and ignominious human impulses—those thoughts and feelings we are most likely to hide from others. The long-running popularity of *Seinfeld*, for example (consistently number one in the ratings despite the fact that its characters and setting are not what Middle America likes to think of as the norm) may well be due to its relentless verbalization of thoughts and feelings we all share and usually refuse to admit, even to ourselves. The laughter it provokes is not only cleansing but liberating, for it says to share these foibles is to be human, and trying to hide them a waste of energy.

The demands made on modern relationships are due partly to the shift from village communities to suburban-type environments. This was striking in an industrial city I once visited in Guyana. The city, divided in two by a large mining operation and tailings pond, was divided socially as well. One half was inhabited entirely by workers, almost all black. The other half was where the managers lived—about two-thirds white at the time but becoming progressively less so. In the workers' half the streets were filled with people at night, talking and laughing in groups—groups who mediated, like a Greek chorus, conflicts that often began within the small houses but were immediately brought outside. The managers' half of the city, however, could have been a wealthy Connecticut suburb. The houses were set back in the trees and scarcely visible. No one was outside. At night one could barely tell if the houses were inhabited. In such a setting, with so little in the way of community ties to mediate or provide support, the demands made on the marital bond are necessarily much higher.

My earlier discussion of these strains assumed a more or less traditional marriage, since two-career families were largely limited to academia. But within a decade the women's movement was in full swing, and women began entering the workforce in large numbers—many simply from economic need but many by preference. The comment that change may lead to one partner "outgrowing" the other applies with even greater force to women who "find themselves" in a professional career, and discover that their husbands have lost relevance in the process.

The child-rearing process is still the main drag on temporary systems. Children often suffer from a lack of stability in their human and physical environments, and while the growth of electronic communication has reduced the necessity for people to move about constantly, the "serial monogamy" aspect of marriage shows no signs of decreasing. Yet this may not have as negative an impact as we then imagined. Although not every child today has rotating parents, there is certainly very little stigma attached to those who do, and where serial monogamy exists it has created a new form of extended family. The son of a friend of mine, for example, who had lived with his

father through mos_ _____ _n wedding that
all his father's former loves be _ _____ since all had been
important to his growth and developmen_

We are in a period of transition between an old system and a new one and every strain and discomfort is heightened by comparison with old assumptions. But human beings are amazingly adaptable and creative, and new systems are in the process of evolving. More fathers are becoming full-time parents, for example, with the result that many children are getting far more fathering than ever existed under traditional arrangements. And will the greater independence forced on children in the two-career family be a loss? Will its effect be any worse than the exaggerated involvement of the bored housewife of the 1950s, expressing her frustrated ambition vicariously through over-identification with her child's development? It may take several generations for these questions to be answered definitively, but it is important to remember that throughout history most men and women have been fully occupied during the working day, leaving their children to grow and develop with other children, intervening only to feed, rest, and occasionally teach them. A method that has existed throughout history is not necessarily the best that can be had, but it is scarcely cause for alarm.

⎯⎯⎯◉⎯⎯⎯

Social change brings pain and costs as well as relief and benefits, perhaps in necessarily equal amounts. In Chapter Three Bennis predicted a society in which temporary systems would be the rule rather than the exception. What would life be like in such a society? How would people relate to one another? Would this further accentuate conditions already present in our society? Or would it create patterns and problems that are altogether new?[2]

One obvious effect of the widespread extension of temporary systems would be a sharp increase in job mobility. If task forces are to be organized on a temporary basis around specific problems, there is no particular reason why their formation should be locally restricted.

Individuals will be brought together on the basis of talent and availability, and geographic location will be less of an impediment than prior commitments. We will become increasingly a nation of itinerants, moving continually on an irregular and perhaps even non-recurrent circuit of jobs. What is mildly characteristic of the academic world and the large corporation today will become accelerated and general throughout the economy. Thus while temporary systems may make work more meaningful, will not the reverse be true of private life?

We know something about the effects of mobility, for we live already in the most mobile society that has ever existed. It is true that there have been many societies that continually moved from place to place. But these nomadic tribes moved as a group, and usually over a fixed route. They carried their possessions, their relationships, their entire way of life along with them, unchanged. In most cases, even the land did not really change, since every part of the route was reencountered at predictable intervals, save in times of climatic or military cataclysm (which though they make history, are grossly unrepresentative). Nomadic tribes are just as rooted to the land as a peasant farmer, but to a corridor instead of a site.

Mobility in modern society is quite another matter. Here individuals or family units are plucked out of their social context and transplanted. They may never live in the same place twice. While they may stay within the same society (and even these boundaries may weaken in the future), they must form new relationships, adapt to a new physical environment, new norms, and so on. Those who remain behind must repair the social fissure that the transients have created.

The consequences of mobility for our culture have been profound. George Pierson has argued with great force that most of what is distinctively American can be traced to it. Optimism, conservatism, other-directedness, individualism, equalitarianism, superficiality, identity-diffusion, gregariousness, alienation, homogeneity, money-mindedness, loneliness, nostalgia, anxiety, conformity, activity, achievement-orientation, pragmatism, love of novelty, materialism, youth-worship—all these real or imagined qualities bear some relationship to the tendency of modern Americans to uproot themselves at relatively frequent intervals.[3]

But we must distinguish between these characteristics that spring directly from the effects of mobility itself, and those created by mechanisms designed to soften these effects. Thus frequent moving about tends to detach the individual from enduring and significant relationships—this is a primary effect. But the difficulty of continually forming new bonds and breaking old ones can be mitigated by developing ways of accelerating the process of acquaintance: an informality, an easy friendliness, a capacity for ready, if superficial ties. This would be a secondary effect—one that need not automatically occur but one that might evolve as a compensatory mechanism.

Primary Consequences of Temporary Systems

We can hypothesize two primary and three secondary consequences of increased mobility and temporary systems, all of them little more than an extrapolation from existing conditions. First, the process of individuation—the separation of the individual from those permanent groups that provide him with ready-made values and traits and from which he derives his identity, will accelerate. His ability to say "I am a such-and-such" prior to the completion of his education or training will disappear. His experience will become more particularized, his knowledge and work more narrowly specialized, his social existence more atomized.

The second effect will be concomitant feelings—acute and pervasive—of alienation, of anomie, of meaninglessness. These feelings will, as usual, be misconstrued as an effect of everyone's having become alike, although the striving toward uniformity is actually a secondary phenomenon, an attempt to *counteract* feelings of alienation and anomie. On the contrary, these feelings arise when the individual is deprived of a permanent contextual group toward whom he feels a bond of likeness heightened by one or two points of specialization that define his role in that group.

Human beings are all equipped with the same emotional repertoire, the same basic needs, the same basic defenses. Out of these they evolve more idiosyncratic structures that we call personality or, when they are based on shared definitions of meaning, culture. These differences help maintain boundaries between individuals and between groups, but at the cost of some violence to the emotional life of the individual. His body may tell him, as a human being, to respond in a given way to a punch in the nose, or a sexual stimulus, or a loss, or a rejection, but he may have learned, as a member of a specific culture or as one playing a special role within that culture, not to react in this human way, but rather in some way that defines him uniquely.

To be more individual, in other words, is to be less human, more of a social artifact. One man learns to lose the capacity to respond to life situations with love, another man with anger, another with jealousy, another with tears, and so on. This process of emotional crippling we call personality development. Its positive side is the hypertrophy of other responses, which permits a kind of emotional specialization within the group. In a permanent group the individual can sense his likeness with others, while the self-alienation that arises from his specialized response system is mitigated by his close and constant contact with other specialists who express his needs and feelings for him as he does for them. In a culture in which a man cannot weep, his women may weep for him. If he is a group jester, there will be some dour compatriot to feel gloomy for him, and so on. And where the group as a whole warps human feeling in a given direction, defining its differentness from other groups, his similarity with those around him palliates his sense of alienation from his feelings.

When an individual loses a more or less permanent role in a permanent group, his specialization becomes pointless and somewhat burdensome. He becomes a part in search of a whole, feeling neither enough like others to avoid a sense of being alone and lost, nor sufficiently included in a stable pattern of differentiation to have a sense of himself as a distinguishable entity embedded in a pattern of other such entities. In a society that places a value on individualism this inability to experience oneself leads paradoxically to a cry for *more* uniqueness, more eccentricity, more individuation, thus exacerbating the symptoms.[4]

The only conceivable solution to this problem is, to put it bluntly, the obliteration of differences: the maximization of uniformity, of homogeneity, of sameness among people. The viability of this solution, however, rests on two assumptions. The first assumption is that we accept mobility as given. It might be felt that the price paid for mobility, for flexibility, for democracy in fact, is too high—that we should try to find ways to bring the entire movement of our times to a sudden and grinding halt before everything of value in human life is lost. I do not regard this as possible, nor am I certain it is desirable. Before settling for the manifold ills that mankind has borne throughout history we owe ourselves the resolution at least to peer into the unknown and imagine what it might hold and what might be made of it.

The second assumption is the more crucial, for if it is not made, few people would wish to accept the first. Homogenization could only be tolerated if people were all transformed into full human beings rather than remaining specialized semi-persons as we are now constituted. Fantasies of uniformity have always made the negative assumption that such uniformity would be based on some kind of personality constriction—that all humans would become robots, or assume the specialized posture of a gregarious suburbanite, or a submissive peasant, or a Prussian officer. We imagine with horror everyone being forced to accept some narrow stance now adopted by a few. But such a homogenization would not be viable, since (1) it would retain the same constraints under which we now suffer without providing the compensatory assurance that others will express vicariously the stunted sides of ourselves; and (2) the advantages of a social division of labor would be lost, and the society as a whole would suffer from the loss of variety, the lack of human resources. Attempts to evolve this kind of uniformity may be (and are being) made, but a society so structured will fail. A viable society must somehow avail itself of a great variety of contradictory human responses. If members of that society are to be limited in the ways they can respond, then each must be limited in different ways—otherwise generalized shortages will (and do) arise. Conversely, if a society is to function with uniform participants, each one must be individually complex and comprehensive in his available response patterns. Each must have the capacity to be introverted *and* extraverted, controlled *and* spontaneous, independent *and* dependent, gregarious *and* seclusive, loving *and* hostile, strong *and* weak, and so on.

This is, of course, utopian. Human beings will never achieve this degree of humanness; nor, happily, will complete uniformity ever be achieved. I am merely saying that insofar as uniformity is sought, specialization and incompleteness must be eschewed. Less variety from person to person requires more variety within each person. The individual will be more changeable, less predictable from moment to moment and from situation to situation, less able to play the same tune all his life long. Wardrobes, taken as a whole, may be more similar, but each one will be far more diversified, and the variety of dress in any given social situation much greater than today.

Secondary Consequences of Temporary Systems

Interchangeability

The first secondary consequence has already been dealt with indirectly. If one must make and break relationships rapidly then it becomes increasingly important that people be as interchangeable as possible, and this is most simply achieved through uniformity.[5] It is, of course, a basic principle of mass production, and has extended itself in a variety of ways throughout our culture, leading to complaints of dullness and monotony. One revealing expression of the principle is the motel. An American today can travel almost anywhere in the country and stop at a motel to find himself in an entirely familiar environment. He would, indeed, be hard put to distinguish one from another. As relationships become increasingly temporary the need to establish such instant familiarity will correspondingly increase.

But people are not motels. We have already pointed out the necessity for an enrichment of the individual before interchangeability will be viable. No such problem exists for the motel: the human need for variety in physical surroundings is extremely limited, even trivial, and we may expect the monotony of our physical environment to maintain its accelerative rate of growth, only slightly damped by self-conscious remedial measures.

Interchangeability is a threatening concept. It violates every principle of association known to man and conjures up an image of social chaos. Yet it is only a logical extension of the evolution of associational principles up to this moment. To understand this point we must undertake a brief but rather abstract digression.

The most primitive and elemental principle of association is territoriality, which simply states that the greater the physical distance between A and B, the less important they are to each other. It exists in pure form almost nowhere at the human level, and almost everywhere at the animal level.[6] Although alloyed with other principles it is still of vital importance in human society. If we make the necessary modification of adding propinquity of *pathways* to static propinquity, it is still the most powerful single factor in human relationships, from marital choice to interfamilial relationships. It lingers as an important bond even when the propinquity is made artificial by temporal separation. Margaret Mead points out that Americans feel linked if they have been in the same location at different times.[7]

The limitations of territoriality are obvious: it is impossible to construct any large-scale organization on this principle alone since there is no way to achieve centralization. Village A can relate to village C only through intermediate village B, while B can relate to D only through C, and so on. There is no basis for assigning greater weight to one village than another. Territoriality forms a seamless web.

But all existing human societies, however primitive, share at least one other associational principle which redresses this deficiency. This principle is kinship, which states that the greater consanguineal distance (defined, somewhat arbitrarily, by each culture) between A and B, the less important they are to each other. This principle is modeled after the territorial one, but is liberated from dependence upon the physical environment. When it is combined with exogamous marriage rules it cuts across the territorial principle, permitting multiple loyalties and the coalescence of larger social units. A populous clan scattered over many villages provides a basis for centralization.

Both of these principles are universal today, but in modern urban societies they have been severely intruded upon by a third.[8] This principle, which we might crudely label the principle of common interest, states that the fewer the interests shared by A and B, the less important they are to each other (the interests may, but need not, be utilitarian). It goes further than kinship in detaching association from fixed external conditions. While the kinship principle is based partly on heredity and partly on cultural definitions, the common-interest principle is entirely cultural, and hence is totally manipulable in cultural terms. It not only permits still larger and more complex social systems, but it also adds an element of flexibility: territories and kin relationships cannot change much, but interests can and do.

The growth of temporary systems will tend to limit further the spheres of territoriality and kinship, and the concept of interchangeability will inaugurate what we might call the principle of temporary relevance. It is not really new, but merely an extension of the common-interest principle. It eliminates *any fixed basis* for human relationships, although the temporary bases derive from common interest. Thus any permanence in human association in the future will depend upon the survival of the two more primitive principles.[9]

Now it can be seen from this progression that each principle frees human relationships more and more from dependence upon external constraints, permitting more freedom of choice and a wider range of possible encounters. What is threatening about interchangeability is first, the introduction of impermanence as a necessary rather than accidental feature of social life and, second, the apparent violation of our popular belief that people relate to one another on the basis of the intrinsic qualities of the other person. The first threat is a real one, which we will discuss later in detail. The second is, in large part, illusory, based on a sentimental misconception of social relationships.

For, obviously, the principles of territoriality and kinship ignore the intrinsic qualities of the other individual altogether. This is expressed in a number of homilies to the effect that one can choose one's friends but not one's relatives or neighbors (the latter is only partially true today). Choice is thus offered as a sop to compensate for the loss of stability, security, and permanence. The choice is not really an individual one, however, and is in that sense an illusion. We are conditioned by our culture and by our early childhood experiences to make certain kinds of choices with fair predictability. Our interest patterns bring us into contact with similar individuals whom we then "choose." The principle of temporary relevance faces up to this reality with rather brutal honesty.

It must be stressed that total interchangeability will never be achieved. If it could be, temporary systems would not be necessary, for they assume at least a technical specialization. But such temporary working groups will have little else in common besides their task. They cannot serve as a social circle, nor will it be easy to enter and leave other circles on so rapid a basis, at least as they are now constituted. It will be increasingly necessary to take people as one finds them—to relate immediately, intensely, and without traditional social props, rituals, and distancing mechanisms. Distance will be provided by transience, and the old patterns of gamesmanship, of extended, gradual, and incomplete unmasking will become inappropriate. By the time the individual reaches his "here-is-the-real-me" flourish, he will find himself alone again. It seems clear that one of the unintended functions of "sensitivity training" or "basic encounter" groups is anticipating a world of temporary systems, since these groups emphasize openness, feedback, immediacy, communication at a feeling level, the here-and-now, more awareness of and ability to express deeper feelings, and so on.[10] Members of such groups often express surprise and chagrin at their capacity to respond with warmth and intensity to individuals they would in other situations have regarded with indifference, fear, or contempt. After the initial shock has worn off the old preference hierarchy is rediscovered, but there remains a sense of how often opportunities for significant relationships are wasted by casual stereotyping. Such an awareness would be a precondition of a society of temporary systems.

Other-Directedness

Another secondary consequence of temporary systems would be the development of more flexible moral patterns. This again represents the intensification of an existing trend rather than a new departure. Mobility and change rule out the efficacy of any permanent system of social control. *External controls* depend upon the permanent embeddedness of the individual in the same social unit—a condition that has largely vanished from the civilized world. *Internalized controls of a fixed kind* rapidly become irrelevant to a changing social environment. Our society has long required, and obtained, a system of internalized controls that incorporates moral relativism—what David Riesman has called "other-direction."[11] The individual must at one and the same time be capable of self-restraint while recognizing that groups vary in what they consider desirable and undesirable social behavior. He must be acutely sensitive and responsive to group norms while recognizing the essential arbitrariness, particularity, and limited relevance of all moral imperatives.

reason that there has been a decrease in the entry of educated women into the professions.

Yet the decline in the specialization of marital roles accompanying mobility constitutes a powerful force for feminine parity, and a mobile society must either accept the pull of competing careers or the push of feminine discontent. Our society has tended, with some ambivalence, toward the latter, and the result has been (in addition to much outcry, argument, and public discussion) an exaggerated investment of feminine energy and ambition into the child-rearing process. While the social costs of either solution are high, it is difficult to envision a more serious social risk than that which results from children having to validate their mothers' competence through their own successes, creativity, and mental health.

The problem of the working mother is usually discussed as if the mother's presence in the home were an unalloyed blessing, which one should attempt to maximize.[20] Child rearing, however, has never been, throughout history, either a full-time or a one-person task, but the adjunct of an otherwise full life; the mother's eccentricities have not been magnified by constant and intense interaction with the child. The child, meanwhile has been his own hero, not merely the central character in his mother's drama, and although he may have been pushed to achieve, his achievement was more clearly his own. The current fervor for such innovations as teaching preschool children to read and compute is quite another matter. This achievement is a triumph for the mother; it expresses *her* ability, her child-rearing and training skills, her worth as a parent. It proves that the middle-class mother's college education and her sacrifice of a career were not wasted. The child is merely a manikin on which her maternal virtues can be displayed. To find out why college students talk so much about identity, lose their motivation to study, drop out, or worry about finding themselves, one need only observe the fanaticism of a group of suburban mothers making sure their children get the right start in nursery school, harassing teachers, hounding their teenagers to study, or trying to get them into college. Once away from home the college student's only reason for existing has suddenly been removed from the immediate environment, and his motivational structure must be completely reorganized. No one ever asks the victims of this now rather typical American pattern of vicarious maternal living whether they might not have preferred to see a little less of their mothers and let both mother and child win their own A's.

But even if this problem could somehow be eliminated, pressures on the marital bond through time would remain. It is not merely a question of the executive outgrowing the wife. The male who participates intensively in a series of temporary systems would be changed by each, and each would make a different set of emotional demands upon him. Different aspects of his personal repertory would be exaggerated or muted in each new system, and his wife would somehow be forced to adapt to these in the context of maintaining the one stable and permanent adult relationship in both their lives.

As noted earlier, contemporary transformations in social relationships largely take the form of converting spatial patterns into temporal ones.[21] The idea of temporary systems itself assumes such a conversion. For as routine tasks become automated, those requiring human participation will increasingly relate to the boundaries of current experience—to invention, ambiguity, unusual synthesis, catastrophic changes, and so on. This means that the skills required will include larger quantities of creativity, imagination, social perception, and personal insight, and will hence draw upon all layers of the personality with maximum involvement and commitment. Such involvement will tend to drive other social affiliations out—temporary systems will inherently be what Lewis Coser calls "greedy organizations"[22]—but only temporarily so. Instead of partial commitment to a relatively large number of groups over a relatively long period of time, we will see relatively total commitment to a single group over a short time period—the organizational equivalent of "serial monogamy" (in which a person may have several spouses but only one at a time) replacing a kind of organizational polygamy.

The metaphor reminds us that some sociologists have imagined the marital relationship in our society to be undergoing a similar alteration—decreasing its stability as it increases its intensity. Time imposes a limit previously maintained by other important relationships (kin, neighborhood, friendship). Is this the pattern that will become characteristic of the future? Will the serial monogamy of adolescent "going steady" relationships become a model for the entire society? Will marriage itself become a temporary system, tied to a particular locality and task?

The principal barrier to this solution is the child-rearing process. It is, in fact, difficult to imagine ways of integrating the raising of children with temporary systems. Not only the constant separations and changes of parents, but even the geographical moves themselves, would have damaging consequences. For our society is one that depends upon the autonomy of the childhood peer group as a way of "quarantining" cohorts. If this were not so, a child moving from place to place with his family would not suffer the social impairment that we know he does in the United States. Peer group relations are simply too important, and the child who must continually make and break them is operating with an enormous handicap.

But this is assuming a transitional state in which some individuals are operating under the new system and some under the old. What if *everyone* were geared to temporary systems and interchangeability? Then every boy in the neighborhood would be the new boy, or would very recently have been, and every child would have rotating parents. Could children adjust to such a general state of affairs, or would it produce shallow, superficial, unreliable, "psychopathic" adults?[23] Would the society then become transformed into something totally different? Would such individuals care about the kinds of issues we are concerned with here? Would it matter if they did not? We must be careful not to treat as inherently destructive those conditions that generate deviant behavior in our own society—not to impose upon the limitless opportunities of the future the warped basic assumptions of the present. Could a world of superficial, fickle, unscrupulous, but nonaggressive individuals make the world any more dangerous than it is or threaten the demise of culture any more? All we can say with any confidence about the assumptions under which we normally operate is that they have enabled us to manipulate the environment a good deal and to make the earth almost uninhabitable. Objective comparison between the joys and dangers of primitive as against civilized life invariably ends in a toss-up.

We can reasonably assume, from what social scientists have found, that the more the infant child is initially dependent upon a small number of nurturing agents the more disturbing will be their loss; loss of the mother between six months and a year probably interferes with the development of personality characteristics necessary for adequate functioning in a mobile society;[24] and any attempt to meet the problem of multiple parents (one assumes the child would normally remain with the mother) by reducing the father's participation in the child-rearing process will generate serious difficulties for male personality development.[25] If these dangers can be averted the viability of a temporary family system is simply an open question.

One must remember, however, that new social mechanisms do not emerge full-blown but evolve from old ones. One can object to any hypothetical social arrangement on the grounds that the transition to it would be intolerable, leading to attempts to thwart and counteract the direction of change. This seems highly likely in the case of the kinds of trends I have been predicting. It is hard to conceive of any mixture of the old and new family systems juxtaposed here that would not be considerably more disturbing than either one in a pure form. Resistance to the transition will produce unusual hybrids that we cannot possibly envision now.

We might also anticipate an increase in opposition to those basic assumptions that precipitate technological change in our society. There will be more questioning of the utilitarian axioms of our lives as the traditional ideas of progress continue to tarnish, and as some underdeveloped countries, operating with different assumptions, leapfrog into a less cluttered and more satisfying modernity. There will be even more emphasis on hedonistic, experience-oriented approaches to life, with or without drugs. There will be more nostalgia, more revivals, more clinging to real and imagined pasts. There will be more world-rejecting fantasies of static, loving, bucolic utopian communities, many of which will be carried into action.[26]

We cannot begin to weight these factors properly and to imagine into what combinations they will be molded. What I have tried to do in this chapter is to suggest some of the forces at work in generating change, some of the strains that they must inevitably create, and some hypothetical solutions to what are fundamentally insoluble dilemmas of social life.

New Patterns of Leadership
for Adaptive Organizations

The opportunity to revisit something you wrote over thirty years ago is one that is both wondrous and unsettling. On one hand, you can bask in a blissful, narcissistic haze with your clever phrases or forecasts. On the other, alas, you can shudder with embarrassment at a brazenly clumsy pronouncement, stated with the certainty of a papal bull and wish, in retrospect, that you had qualified or softened the tone, or better, dropped it completely.

Oh well, just thank the Lord for having an opportunity to retract or amplify. The French have a phrase for this: *"l'esprit d'escalier,"* literally, the spirit of the staircase—the things we wish we had said as we walk down the steps *after* a meeting. Here I have a chance to say two things that I wish I had said in the first incarnation of this book. I'd like to start with a quote taken from the chapter, one written with all the bravado and hubris that goes with youth:

> Accepted theory and conventional wisdom concerning leadership have a lot in common. Both say that the success of a leader depends on the leader, the led, and the unique situation. This formulation, abstract and majestically useless, is the best that can be gleaned from more than one hundred years of research on the problem of leadership. How inadequate and pallid formulations are when compared to the myths and primitive psychological issues surrounding such complexities as leadership and power. . . .

Immediately after that quote, I segued off into the outer blue, blithely ignoring my admonition about the deeper, archaic and psychological complexities I glibly threw to the reader. So I wish I had written more about *character* back then, something that's fascinated me and that I've written about in more recent (and I hope, wiser) years.

As I see it now, leadership *is* character and the process of becoming a leader is much the same as becoming an integrated human being. The word *character* itself is interesting. It's from the Greek, meaning *engraved* and from the French for *inscribed*. It has to do with who we are as human beings, our nature, cosmology and what shaped us. Character is basically about how we organize and conceptualize our experiences. Unlike the classical Freudian outlook, I don't think our character is totally formed at age six or seven or eight or even eighty. Character continuously evolves; it grows and develops over our lifetime.

Now when you look at the typical criteria that most organizations use to evaluate their executives and managers, there are usually seven. These seven are not always explicit, and some are more heavily weighted than others, but they are always present in some form or another: (1) technical competence, sometimes called business literacy, (2) people skills, (3) conceptual skills, (4) track record/results, (5) taste (choosing good people), (6) judgment, and (7) character.

Now what's interesting about the last two—judgment and character—is that they are the most difficult to identify, measure, or develop. Recent research by A. J. Slywotzky and D. S. Morrison shows that 85 percent of success or failure at work can be explained by character.[1] We certainly don't know much about teaching those competencies. Business schools barely try. We do know something about how they're formed and developed but not quite enough to be confident about how they're imparted. What's important and poignant is that it's rare to find a case where an executive is de-railed or plateaued for lack of technical competence. The most common cause of a career stopper is lack of judgment and character (usually cloaked in such terms as questions about "integrity" or trust or inter-personal deficits).

The second thing I wish I had spent more time considering in the first edition was the significance of *intellectual capital*—a portman-teau term that includes ideas, brainpower, know-how, imagination, innovation—well, you get the idea. In self-defense, intellectual cap-ital was hinted at when Phil and I exalted the role of science and technology and their significance in organizational life. But it was never limned or emphasized sufficiently. And now I can't think of anything *more* significant than intellectual capital for any organiza-tion that wants to be in the phone book by the year 2000. I see this as the single most important part of any leader's job description: the capacity to generate and release the brainpower of the workforce. This is what matters most. The frustrating thing is that intellectual capital is hard to measure.

Not long ago, the *New York Times* ran a rhapsodic front-page story about the IBM takeover of Lotus—a $3.5 billion acquisition. One paragraph in particular interested me: "Perhaps the most striking aspect of IBM's takeover bid, and the one that says the most about these times, is that it defies the accepted wisdom on the difficulties of trying to acquire a company whose primary value isn't in its machin-ery or real estate but rather in that most mercurial of assets—peo-ple." More graphically, Bill Gates said in a recent interview that the "only factory asset Microsoft has is human imagination."

The best and brightest leaders know this. Disney's Michael Eisner, especially when he refers to the feature animation troupe, says that "my inventory goes home every night." As if more evidence were needed to make this point, a University of Pennsylvania study by Robert Zemsky of 3,200 U.S. firms shows that a 10 percent increase of education of the workforce leads to an 8.5 percent increase in pro-ductivity, whereas a 10 percent increase in capital expenditures leads to a 3.8 percent increase in productivity.

So as I walk down (or up) the staircase thirty years later, I wish I had said a little more about the importance of character and intel-lectual capital.

In the United States a man builds a house to spend his latter years in it, and he sells it before the roof is on; he plants a garden, and lets it just as the trees are coming into bearing; he brings a field into tillage and leaves other men to gather the crops; he embraces a profession and gives it up; he settles in a place, which he soon afterward leaves, to carry his changeable longings elsewhere. If his private affairs leave him any leisure, he instantly plunges into the vortex of politics; and if at the end of a year of unremitting labor, he finds he has a few days vacation, his eager curiosity whirls him over the vast extent of the United States, and he will travel fifteen hundred miles in a few days to shake off his happiness. Death at length overtakes him, but it is before he is weary of his bootless chase of that complete felicity which is forever on the wing.[2]

What we have been emphasizing in the past two chapters—modern man's capacity and need for temporary, fleeting relationships and structures—was spotted long ago by that restless Frenchman, de Tocqueville. What he could not foresee was the rapid contagion of mobility as industrialization spread, and he would undoubtedly be alternately amused and horror-struck by the realization of his observations in France of 1968. In Chapter Four we focused on the consequences of temporary, nonpermanent relationships in purely human terms. Now we can revert to Chapter Three and ask about the consequences of temporary systems on organizational behavior, particularly how it affects the leadership and authority of these organizations.

The key word for describing their structures is *temporary*. There will be adaptive, rapidly changing *temporary systems*. These will be task forces composed of groups of relative strangers with diverse professional backgrounds and skills organized around problems to be solved. The groups will be arranged on an organic rather than mechanical model, meaning that they will evolve in response to a problem rather than to preset, programmed expectations. People will be evaluated, not vertically according to rank and status but flexibly according to competence. Organizational charts will consist of project groups rather than stratified functional groups.

Most of these trends have been surfacing for some years in the aerospace, construction, drug, and consulting industries as well as in professional and research and development organizations. Living at a time and place where rapid social and technological change is endemic, it should not be surprising if the future invades overnight, before the forecast is fully comprehended.

A question left unanswered in Chapter Three had to do with the leadership of these new-style organizations. How would they be managed? Are there any guidelines transferable from present managerial practices? Do the behavioral sciences provide any suggestions for leaders of the future? How can these complex, ever-changing, free-form, kaleidoscopic patterns be coordinated? Of course, there can be no definitive answers to these questions until the direction of the future emerges. At the same time, unless we attempt to understand the leadership requirements for the future, we shall inevitably back into it rather than manage it effectively.

Accepted theory and conventional wisdom concerning leadership have a lot in common. Both say that the success of a leader depends on the leader, the led, and the unique situation. This formulation, abstract and majestically useless, is the best that can be gleaned from more than one hundred years of research on the problem of leadership. How inadequate and pallid formulations are when compared to the myths and primitive psychological issues surrounding such complexities as leadership and power. Our preoccupation with the Kennedys and Lyndon Johnson is more than idol curiosity; leadership theory coexists with a powerful and parallel primitive reality. It is the latter reality, archetypal and mythic, that we hope to upset by raising fears that our admirable ancestor and archetype— the aggressive, inner-directed nineteenth-century autocrat—will become obsolete. We will return to this point later on. At the moment, let us quickly review some of the key situational features confronting the leader of the future.

Situational Features

The overarching feature is change itself, its accelerating rate and its power to transform. The phrase "the only constant is change" has reached the point of being a cliché, which at once anesthetizes us to its pain and stimulates grotesque fantasies about life in a brave new world with no place in the sun. Change is the "godhead" term for our age as it has not been for any other. One must recall that the British Parliament was debating in the last part of the nineteenth century whether to close up the Royal Patent Office as all significant inventions had already been made.

What are the most salient changes affecting human organization, the ones with most relevance to their governance? Foremost is the changing nature of our institutions. In 1947, employment stood at approximately 58 million and now is at about 72 million. "Virtually all of this increase occurred in industries that provide services, e.g., banks, hospitals, retail stores, and schools."[3] This nation has become the only country to employ more people in services than in production of tangible goods. Today the growth industries, if we can call them that, are education, health, welfare, and other professional institutions. The problem facing organizations is no longer manufacturing—it is the management of large-scale, socio-technical systems and the strategic deployment of high-grade professional talent.[4]

There are other important obstacles and consequences of change. For example, the working population will be *younger, smarter,* and more *mobile*. In one year, half of our country's population will be under twenty-five, and at the present time one out of every three persons is fifteen years of age or younger. More people are going to college; more than half from certain urban areas go to college. The U.S. Post Office Department reported that one out of every five families changes its address every year.

Most of these changes compel us to look beyond bureaucracy for newer models of organizations that have the capability to cope with contemporary conditions. The general direction of these changes— toward more service and professional organizations, toward more educated, younger, and mobile employees, toward more diverse, complex, science-based systems, toward a more turbulent and uncertain environment—forces us to consider new styles of leadership. Leading the enterprise of the future becomes a significant social process, requiring as much managerial as substantive competence. Robert S. McNamara is a case in point. Before coming to Washington, he was considered for three cabinet positions: Defense, State, and Treasury. His only recommendation was that he was a superior administrator. Success or failure in the U.S. Department of State also depends as much or more on one's interpersonal and managerial competence as on one's substantive knowledge of "diplomacy."[5] Leadership of modern organizations also depends on new forms of knowledge and skills not necessarily related to the primary task of the organization. In short, the pivotal function in the leader's role has changed from a sole concern with the substantive to an emphasis on the interpersonal.

Main Tasks of Leadership

One convenient focus for a discussion of leadership is to review the main problems confronting modern organizations, presented in Chapter Three, and to understand the kinds of tasks and strategies linked to the solution of these problems. We have summarized these on the following pages and have attempted to show some possible executive steps.

Integration: Developing Rewarding Human Systems

A simple way to understand the problem of integration is to compute the ratio between what an individual gives and what he gets in his day-to-day transactions. In organizational terms, we can ask, Are the *contributions* to the organization about equivalent to the *inducements* received? Where there is a high ratio between inducements and contributions, either the organization or the employee gets restless and searches for more rewarding environments or people.

There is nothing startling or new about this formulation. What is interesting is that organizations frequently do not know what is truly rewarding. This is particularly true for the professionals and highly trained workers who will dominate the organizations of the future. With this class of employee, conventional policies and practices regarding incentives, never particularly sensitive, tend to be inapplicable.

Most organizations regard economic rewards as the primary incentive to peak performance. These are not unimportant to the professional, but—provided economic rewards are equitable—other incentives become far more potent. Avarice, to contradict Hume, is *not* the spur of industry, particularly of professionals. Professionals tend to seek such rewards as full utilization of their talent and training: professional status (not necessarily within the organization but externally with respect to their profession); and opportunities for development and further learning. The main difference between the professional and the more conventional, hourly employee is that the former will not yield career authority to the organization.

The most important incentive, then, is to "make it" professionally, to be respected by professional colleagues. Loyalty to an organization may increase if it encourages professional growth. (I was told recently that a firm decided to build all future plants in university towns in order to attract and hold on to college-trained specialists.) The "good place to work" resembles a super-graduate school, alive with dialogue and senior colleagues, where the employee will not only work to satisfy organizational demands but, perhaps primarily, those of his profession.[6]

The other incentive was mentioned earlier (Chapter Three) when I suggested that people in organizations are looking toward work for self-realization, for personal growth that may not be task-related. That remark questions four centuries of an encrusted Protestant Ethic, reinforced by the indispensability of work for the preservation and justification of existence. But work, as we all must experience it, serves at least two psychic functions: that of binding man more closely to reality and secondly "of displacing a large amount of libidinal components, whether narcissistic, aggressive, or even erotic, on to professional work and on to the human relations connected with it. . . ."[7]

It is not at all clear as to how (or even *if*) these latter needs can be deliberately controlled by the leadership. Company-sponsored courses, T-groups, and other so-called adult education courses may, in fact, reflect these needs. Certainly attitudes toward continuing education are changing. The idea that education has a terminal point and that college students come in only four sizes—18, 19, 20, and 21—is old-fashioned. A dropout should be redefined to mean anyone who hasn't *returned* to school.

Whichever way the problem of professional and personal growth is resolved, it is clear that many of the older forms of incentives, based on lower echelons of the need hierarchy (safety-economic-physiological), will have to be reconstituted. Even more profound will be the blurring of the boundaries between work and play, between affiliative and achievement drives, which nineteenth-century necessities and mores have unsuccessfully attempted to compartmentalize.

Social Influence: Developing Executive Constellations

There are many issues involved in the distribution of power: psychological, practical, and moral. I will consider only the practical side, which has obvious implications for the other two concerns. To begin with, it is quaint to think that one man, no matter how omniscient and omnipotent, can comprehend, to say nothing of control, the diversity and complexity of the modern organization. Followers and leaders who think this is possible get entrapped in a false dream, a child's fantasy of absolute power and absolute dependence.

Today it is hard to imagine that during the Civil War, "government" (Lincoln's executive staff) had fewer than fifty civilian subordinates, and not many executives at that, but chiefly telegraph clerks and secretaries. Even so recent an administration as Franklin Roosevelt's had a cozy, family tone about it. According to his doctor, for example, Roosevelt "loved to know everything that was going on and delighted to have a finger in every pie."[8]

"Having a finger in every pie" may well be an occupational disease of presidents, but it is fast becoming outmoded. Today's administration must reflect the necessities imposed by size and complexity. In fact, there has been a general tendency in business to move away (tacitly) from a presidential form of power to a cabinet or team concept, with some exceptions where team management has been conceptualized (like Union Carbide) and made explicit. There is still a long-standing, pseudo masculine tendency to disparage such plural executive arrangements, but they are informally on the increase.

This system of an executive constellation by no means implies an abdication of responsibility by the chief executive. It should reflect a functionally divided effort based on the distinct competencies of the constellation. It is a way of multiplying executive power through a realistic allocation of effort. Of course, this means also that top executive personnel are chosen not only on the basis of their unique talents but on how complementary and compatible these skills and competencies are.

Despite all the problems inherent in the executive constellation concept—problems of building an effective team, compatibility, and so forth—it is hard to see other valid solutions to the constraints of magnitude and sheer overload of the leader's role.

Collaboration: Building a Collaborative Climate

Related to the problem of developing an effective executive constellation is another key task of the leader—building a collaborative climate. An effective, collaborative climate is easier to experience and harder to achieve than a formal description, but most students of group behavior would agree that it should include the following ingredients: flexible and adaptive structure, utilization of member talents, clear and agreed-upon goals, norms of openness, trust, and cooperation, interdependence, high intrinsic rewards, and trans-actional controls, that is, members of the unit should have a high degree of autonomy and a high degree of participation in making key decisions.

Developing this group "synergy" is difficult, and most organizations take the easy way out: a "zero synergy" strategy. This means that the organization operates under the illusion that it will hire the best individuals in the world and then adopt a Voltairean stance of allowing them to "cultivate their own gardens." This strategy of isolation can best be observed in universities where it operates with great sophistication. Universities are, of course, a special case but until they take a serious look at their "anomic" existence, there is little hope that they will solve their vexing problems. The Berkeley riots were symptomatic of at least four self-contained, uncommunicating social systems (students, faculty, administration, regents) without the trust, empathy, and interaction, to say nothing of tradition, to develop meaningful collaboration. To make matters worse, academics, by nature and reinforced by tradition, see themselves as loners and divergent. They want to be independent together, so to speak. Academic narcissism goes a long way on the lecture platform but may be positively dysfunctional for developing a community.

Another equally pernicious strategy with the same effects but different style (and more typical of American business institutions) is a pseudo democratic "groupiness" where false harmony and conflict-avoidance persist.

Synergy is hard to develop. Lack of experience and strong cultural biases against group efforts worsen the problem. Groups, like other highly complicated organisms, need time to develop. They require time, interaction, trust, communication, and commitment, and these ingredients require a period of gestation. I am as continually amazed at expectation of easy maturity in groups as I would be in young children.

Expensive and time consuming as it is, building synergetic and collaborative cultures will become essential. Modern problems are too complex and diversified for one man or one discipline. They require a blending of skills and perspectives, and only effective problem-solving units will be able to master them.

Adaptation: Identification with the Adaptive Process

In the early days of the last war when armaments of all kinds were in very short supply, the British, I am told, made use of a venerable field piece that had come down to them from previous generations. The honorable past of this light artillery stretched back, in fact, to the Boer War. In the days of uncertainty after the fall of France, these guns, hitched to trucks, served as useful mobile units in the coast defense. But it was felt that the rapidity of fire could be increased. A time-motion expert was, therefore, called in to suggest ways to simplify the firing procedures. He watched one of the gun crews of five men at practice in the field for some time. Puzzled by certain aspects of the procedures, he took some slow-motion pictures of the soldiers performing the loading, aiming, and firing routines.

When he ran those pictures over once or twice, he noticed something that appeared odd to him. A moment before the firing, two members of the gun crew ceased all activity and came to attention for a three-second interval extending throughout the discharge of the gun. He summoned an old colonel of artillery, showed him the pictures, and pointed out this strange behavior. "What," he asked the colonel, "did it mean?" The colonel, too, was puzzled. He asked to see the pictures again. "Ah," he said when the performance was over, "I have it. They are holding the horses."[9]

This story demonstrates nicely the pain with which man accommodates to change. And yet, ironically, he continues to seek out new inventions, which disorder his serenity and undermine his competence.

One striking index of the rapidity of change—for me, the single most dramatic index—is the shrinking interval between the time of a discovery and its commercial application. Before World War I, the lag between invention and utilization was thirty-three years; between World War I and World War II, it was seventeen years. After World War II, the interval decreased to about nine years. The transistor was discovered in 1948, and by 1960, 95 percent of all the important equipment and more than 50 percent of *all* electronic equipment utilized them in place of conventional vacuum tubes. The first industrial application of computers was in 1956.

Modern organizations, even more than individuals, are acutely vulnerable to the problem of responding flexibly and appropriately to new information. Symptoms of maladaptive responses, at the extremes, are (1) a guarded, frozen, rigid response, denying the presence or avoiding the recognition of changes resulting most typically in organizational paralysis; or (2) susceptibility to change resulting in a spastic, unreliable faddism. It is obvious that there are times when openness to change is appropriate and other times when it may be disastrous. Organizations, in fact, should reward people who act as counterchange agents, creating forces against the seduction of newness for its own sake.

How can the leadership of these new-style organizations create an atmosphere of continuity and stability amid an environment of change? Whitehead put the problem well when he said

> The art of society consists first in the maintenance of the symbolic code, and secondly, in the fearlessness of revision. . . . Those societies which cannot combine reverence to their symbols with freedom of revision must ultimately decay. . . .

There is no easy solution to the tension between stability and change. We are not yet an emotionally adaptive society, though we are as close to having to become one as any society in history. Morison suggests in his brilliant essay on change that "we may find at least part of our salvation in identifying ourselves with the adaptive process and thus share some of the joy, exuberance, satisfaction, and security . . . to meet . . . changing times."[10]

The remarkable aspect of our generation is its commitment to change in thought and action. Executive leadership must take responsibility in creating a climate that provides the security to identify with the adaptive process without fear of losing status and self-esteem. Creating an environment that would increase a tolerance for ambiguity and where one can make a virtue out of uncertainty, rather than one that induces hesitancy and its reckless counterpart, expediency, is one of the most challenging tasks for the new leadership.

Identity: Building Supraorganizational Goals and Commitments

Organizations, like individuals, suffer from identity crises. They are not only afflictions that attack during adolescence, but chronic states pervading every phase of organizational development. The new organizations we speak of, with their bands of professional pseudo-species, coping within a turbulent environment, are particularly allergic to problems of identity. Professional and regional orientations lead frequently to fragmentation, intergroup conflicts and power plays, and rigid compartmentalization, devoid of any unifying sense of purpose or mission.

The university is a wondrous place for advanced battle techniques, far overshadowing its business counterparts in subterfuge and sabotage. Quite often a university becomes a loose collection of competing departments, schools, institutes, committees, centers, and programs, largely noncommunicating because of the multiplicity of specialist jargons and interests and held together, as Robert Hutchins once said, chiefly by a central heating system, or as Clark Kerr amended, by questions of what to do about the parking problem.

The modern organizations we speak of are composed of men who love independence as fiercely as the ancient Greeks, but it is also obvious that they resist what every Athenian, as a matter of course, gave time and effort for: "building and lifting up the common life."

Thucydides has Pericles saying:

> We are a free democracy. . . . We do not allow absorption in our own affairs to interfere with participation in the city's. We regard men who hold aloof from public affairs as useless; nevertheless we yield to none in independence of spirit and complete self-reliance.[11]

A modern version of the same problem (which the Greeks couldn't solve either, despite the lofty prose) has been stated by the president of a large university:

> The problem with this institution is that too few people understand or care about the overall goals. Typically they see the world through their own myopic departmental glasses; i.e., too constricted and biased. What we need more of are professional staff who can wear not only their own school or departmental "hat" but the overall university hat.

Having heard variations of this theme over the years, a number of faculty and administrators, who thought they could "wear the overall university hat" formed in one institution what later came to be known as "the hats group." They came from a variety of departments and hierarchical levels and represented a rough microcosm of the entire university. The hats group continued to meet over the past several years and played an important role in influencing university policy.[12]

First, it can identify and support those individuals who can serve as articulating points between various groups and departments.

There are many individuals who have a bicultural facility, a capacity for psychological and intellectual affinity with different languages and cultures. Organizations are composed of subcultures or "tribes," and such individuals, called "linking pins" in the literature of organization theory, can play a vital role in keeping open the passages of communication.[13]

There is an interesting analogy to this same problem in today's "multiversity." The intellectual disciplines are burrowing deeper into their own narrowing spheres of interest. The American Psychological Association, for example, has been considering some sort of dissolution of its present omnibus structure into smaller, more homogeneous specialties. Other disciplines have or will face the same problem. Yet, the most interesting problems turn up at the intersection between disciplines, and it may take an outsider to identify these. The separate disciplines go their crazy-quilt way and rely more and more on dubious internal standards of validity and competence. As we have moved away in American education from the broad, humanistic, general-education style of the English universities to the German, science-oriented, disciplinary education, we have become rather clumsy and impressionable when confronted with problems out of our own field, and likely to be opinionated in a speculative way. And where something is to be done we become curiously indecisive, ready to place the burden of obligation on someone else who can supply a more-informed judgment.[14]

The problem with a good deal of intellectual effort today is that it lacks a philosopher. Developing a grand synthesis is not a particularly rewarding (or rewarded) activity.

This short detour illustrates the third important function for leadership in developing and shaping identity. Organizations, not only the academic disciplines, require philosophers, individuals who can provide articulation between seemingly inimical interests, who can break down the pseudo-species, transcend vested interests, regional ties, and professional biases. This is precisely what Mary Parker Follett had in mind when she discussed leadership in terms of an ability to bring about a "creative synthesis" between differing codes of conduct.

Chester Barnard in his classic *Functions of the Executive* recognized this, as well as the personal energy and cost of political process. He wrote

> It seems to me that the struggle to maintain cooperation among men should as surely destroy some men morally as battle destroys some physically.[15]

Revitalization: Controlling Destiny

For the leader, revitalization means that the organization has to take a conscious responsibility for its own evolution; that, without a planned methodology and explicit direction, the enterprise will not realize its full potential. For the leader, the issue of revitalization confronts him with the penultimate challenge: growth or decay.

The challenge for the leader is to develop a climate of inquiry and enough psychological and employment security for continual reassessment and renewal. The organizational culture must be developed which enables individuals to

1. Develop a willingness to participate in social revolution against unknown, uncertain, and implacable forces
2. Develop a commitment to collect valid data and to act on limited information without fear of loss of control

The problem of revitalization is connected with the leader's ability to collect valid data, feed it back to the appropriate individuals, and develop action planning on the basis of the data. This three-step "action-research" model of (1) data-generation, (2) feedback, and (3) action planning sounds deceptively simple. In fact, it is difficult. Quite often, the important data cannot be collected by the leader for many obvious reasons. Even when the data are known, there are many organizational short circuits and "dithering devices" which distort and prevent the data from getting to the right places at the right time. And even when steps 1 and 2 are satisfactorily completed, organizational inhibitions may not lead to implementation.

In response to the need for systematic data collection many organizations are setting up "institutional research" centers that act as basic fact-gathering agencies. In some cases, they become an arm of policy making. Mostly, they see as their prime responsibility the collection and analysis of data that bear on the effectiveness with which the organization achieves its goals.

Fact gathering may be a necessary component in revitalization, but it is rarely sufficient by itself to change attitudes and beliefs and to overcome the natural inertia and unnatural resistance to change. Individuals have an awesome capacity to selectively inattend to facts, that may, in their eyes, detract from or threaten their self-esteem. Facts and logic may be the least potent form of influence that man possesses.

Some progressive organizations are setting up organizational development departments that attempt to reduce the "implementation gap" between information and new ideas and action.[16] These OD departments become the center for the entire strategic side of the organization, including not only long-run planning but plans for gaining participation and commitment to the plans. This last step is the most crucial for the guarantee of successful implementation.

New Concepts for Leadership

In addition to substantive competence and comprehension of both social and technical systems, the new leader will have to possess interpersonal skills, not the least of which is the ability to defer his own immediate desires and gratifications in order to cultivate the talents of others. Let us examine some of the ways leadership can successfully cope with the new organizational patterns.

Understanding the "Social Territory"

"You gotta know the territory," sang "Professor" Harold Hill to his fellow salesmen in *The Music Man*. The "social territory" encompasses the complex and dynamic interaction of individuals, roles, groups, organizational and cultural systems. Organizations are, of course, legal, political, technical, and economic systems, but given our purposes we will focus primarily on the social system.

Analytic tools, drawn primarily from social psychology and sociology, are available to aid leadership in the understanding of the social territory. But more than analytic-conceptual tools are needed to augment and implement this understanding. Leadership is as much craft as science. Analytical methods suffice for the latter, but the main instrument or tool for the leader-as-a-craftsman is *himself*, and how creatively he can use his own personality. This is particularly important for leaders to understand, for they, like physicians, are "iatrogenic," that is, physicians are capable of spreading as well as curing disease. And again, like the physician, it is important for the leader to follow the maxim "know thyself" so that he can control some of the pernicious effects he may create unwittingly. Unless the leader understands his actions and effects on others, he may be a carrier rather than a solver of problems.

Thus the leader must be willing and able to set up reliable mechanisms of feedback so that he can not only conceptualize the social territory of which he is an important part, but realize how he influences it.

An Action-Research Model of Leadership

Understanding the social territory and how one influences it is related to the action-research model of leadership mentioned earlier: (1) collection of data, (2) feedback to appropriate sources, and (3) action planning. The "hangup" in most organizations is that people tend to distort and suppress data (particularly in communicating to higher levels) for fear of retaliation or on the basis of other fantasied or real threats. (Samuel Goldwyn, a notorious martinet, called his top staff together after a particularly bad box-office flop and said, "Look, you guys, I want you to tell me exactly what's wrong with this operation and my leadership—even if it means losing your job!")

The Concept of "System-Intervention"

Another aspect of the social territory that has key significance for leadership is the idea of system. For at least two decades, research has been making this point unsuccessfully. Research has shown that productivity can be modified by group norms, that training effects fade out and deteriorate if the training effects are not compatible with the goals of the social system, that group cohesiveness is a powerful motivator, that intergroup conflict is a major problem facing organizations, that individuals take many of their cues and derive a good deal of their satisfaction from their primary work group, that identification with the small work group turns out to be the only stable predictor of productivity, and so on.

The fact that this evidence is so often cited and so rarely acted upon leads one to infer that there is something naturally preferable (on the order of an involuntary reflex) in locating the sources of problems in the individual and diagnosing situations as functions of faulty individuals rather than as symptoms of malfunctioning social systems.[17] What this irrational reflex is based upon is not altogether clear. Superficially, one can argue that pinning the blame or credit on individuals is much easier than identifying system problems, which are, by definition, more complex and abstract. It is simply easier to talk about people than abstractions.

It seems that individuals, living amid complex and subtle organizational conditions, do tend to oversimplify and distort complex realities so that people rather than conditions embody the problem. This tendency toward personalization can be observed in many situations. Illustrations of this can be seen when members of organizations take on familial nicknames, such as "Dad," "Big Brother,"

"Mom," "Mother Hen," "Dutch Uncle," and so on. We can see it in distorted polarizations such as the "good guy" leader and his "hatchet man" assistant. These grotesques seem to bear such little resemblance to the actual people that one has to ask what psychological needs are being served by this complex process of denial and stereotyping.

One answer was hinted at earlier in the Freud quote, where he said that work provides an outlet for displacing emotional components onto professional work and the human relations associated with work. It is clear that an organization is able to absorb an enormous amount of feeling that is projected onto it by its membership. The primitive drama of dreams and childhood can be parlayed into a form of "aesopianism" where individuals, at some distance from the citadels of power, can analyze, distort, stereotype, project, and sublimate all their own deeper wishes and fears into the shadowy reaches of the organization. The recent success of *MacBird* is only one such example of this aesopianism, but it occurs all the time. If there weren't kings and queens we would have to invent them as therapeutic devices to allay anxieties about less romantic, more immediate mothers and fathers, brothers and sisters.

Organizations are big, complex, wondrous, and hamstrung with inertia. Impotence and alienation imprison the best of men, the most glorious of intentions. There is a myth that the higher one goes up the ladder, the more freedom and potency one experiences. In fact, this is frequently not the case, as almost any chief executive will report. Paradoxically, the higher one goes the more tethered and bound he feels by expectations and commitments. In any case, as one gets entrapped by inertia and impotence, it is easier to blame heroes and villains than the system. For if the problems are embroidered into the fabric of the social system, complex as they are, the system can be changed. The effect of locating problems in people rather than systems frequently leads to organizational paralysis because changing human nature often appears to be and frequently is more difficult than changing systems.

Other-Directed Leadership

One famous typology in the social sciences was introduced by David Riesman in his book, *The Lonely Crowd*.[18] He asserted that contemporary man is more "other-directed" than his father—or certainly his grandfather—who would have been characterized as "inner-directed." These character types refer essentially to the ways individuals are influenced and the forces that shape their perspectives. Other-directed man takes his cues from his peer group rather than from his parents. In other words, he takes his relationships more seriously than he does his relatives. His ideology, values, and norms are transmitted to him and accepted by the particular social group that he associates with. He is a "pleaser," cooperative and accommodating. Inner-directed man, to extend an exaggeration, responds to some internal gyroscope, typically, internalized parental pressures. He responds not to any social grouping but to some inner cues—shadowed reflections of his parents' dictates. Inner-directed man is rigid, unyielding, and he acts on principles.

E. E. Lawler and L. W. Porter, as reported in their work on attitudes affecting managerial performance,[19] have been studying inner-directedness and other-directedness in different organizational settings. Previous investigators have always found that organizations tended to reward the aggressive, forceful, decisive, inner-directed leader rather than the cooperative, adaptable, other-directed leader. Their study showed the opposite to be true, that other-directed leaders tend to be rewarded more than inner-directed leaders. They concluded, quite rightly, that the type of organization undoubtedly influences the style of leadership behavior rewarded. Their study was conducted in *service* agencies whereas all previous studies had been undertaken in *industrial* settings.[20]

In light of the fact that our nation has become a truly service-centered society, this finding of Lawler and Porter becomes even more significant. In the growth industries of education, health, welfare, government, and professional organizations, the prime requisites of a leader will be interpersonal competence and other-directedness.

An Agricultural Model of Leadership

I have not found the right word or phrase that accurately portrays the concept of leadership I have in mind, which can be summarized as follows: *an active method for producing conditions where people and ideas and resources can be cultivated to optimum effectiveness and growth*. The phrase "other-directedness," unfortunately, has taken on the negative tone of "exclusively tuned in to outside cues." For a while I thought that "applied biology" might capture the idea, for it connotes an ecological point of view; a process of observation, careful intervention, and organic development. I have also noticed that many biologists and physicians (particularly those physicians who either have not practiced or who went into public health, psychiatry, or research) are excellent administrators. Socrates used a close and congenial metaphor to symbolize the role of the teacher: the midwife, someone who helped others to give birth to creations.

The most appropriate metaphor I have found to characterize adaptive leadership is an "agricultural" model. The leader's job, as I have stated, is to build a climate where growth and development are culturally induced. Roy Ash (1967), an astute industrialist and chairman of Litton Industries, remarked

> If the larger corporations, classically viewed as efficient machines rather than hothouses for fomenting innovation, can become both of these at once, industrial competition will have taken on new dimensions.[21]

I think Ash captures exactly the shift in metaphor I am getting at, from a mechanical model to an organic one. Up until very recent times, the metaphor most commonly used to describe power and leadership in organizations derived from Helmholtz's laws of mechanics. Max Weber, who first conceptualized the model of bureaucracy, wrote

> Bureaucracy is like a modern judge who is a vending machine into which the pleadings are inserted along

with the fee and which then disgorges the judgment with
its reasons mechanically derived from the code.[22]

The language of organizational theory in most contemporary
writings reflects the machine metaphor: social engineering, equi-
librium, friction, resistance, force-field, and so on. The vocabulary
for adaptive organizations requires an organic metaphor, a description of a *process*, not structural arrangements. This process must
include such terms as *open, dynamic systems, developmental, organic,
adaptive*, and so forth.

The key aspect of the process insofar as leadership is concerned
is the ability of the leader to develop a collaborative relationship
with his subordinates. This is not to say that the leader should be a
"good guy" or seek popularity, but it does mean that he will have to
learn to negotiate and collaborate with his subordinates. This is true
for many reasons. In the first place, the leader can't know everything, and his subordinates have the information and competencies
that he needs. In other words, how the leader gets access to and uses
information depends entirely on his ability to collaborate with his
employees (and colleagues, for that matter). While Marx argued
that power accrues to the man with property, we argue that power
accrues to the man who can gather and control information wisely.

In the second place, the psychological "contract" between leader
and led is more satisfying and almost always more productive if the
relationship is more egalitarian. This is particularly true with professionals and a young, intelligent workforce with a "participating
democracy" ideology. D. C. Pelz has shown in his research on scientists and engineers that the most productive research scientists
and engineers are those who work in situations where the processes
of determining work objectives are *transactional* rather than *unilateral*.[23] Pelz used the latter term to describe work relationships where
either the leader (usually a research director) *or* the researcher made
important decisions alone. Transactional arrangements were those
where the leader and researcher reached decisions together—col-

laboratively. What Pelz calls the "deadly condition" is the one in which standards and objectives were imposed by the leader alone, without any voice by the scientists. In the deadly condition, the scientists performed more poorly than in those situations where the scientist decided unilaterally. But neither of the unilateral conditions, where the scientist decided by himself or where the boss decided for him, ever matched the quality of work under the collaborative relationships where decisions were reached through a collaborative process.

Perhaps the most difficult aspect of this style of leadership is to transact (and confront!) those recalcitrant parts of the system that are retarded, stunted, or afraid to grow. This will require enormous energy, saintly patience, and a sophisticated optimism in growth (or a high tolerance for disenchantment).

All these strategic and practical considerations lead to a totally new concept of leadership. The pivotal aspect of this concept is that it relies less on the leader's substantive knowledge about a particular topic than it does on the understanding and possession of skills summarized under the agricultural model. Perhaps a concrete example will help illustrate this. The role of ambassador, or really any U.S. foreign service officer, has evolved to a point where substantive knowledge about a particular geo-political area, such as the Far East or Europe or Latin America, is less important than certain leadership skills similar to the ones I am describing. First of all, the geo-political areas and the substantive knowledge required to understand them change by the month. Second, even if the knowledge base was stable, the ambassador or charge d'affaires could not master it all. Third, and most important, the role of the foreign service officer has become infinitely more complex. He is now at the center of a highly variegated set of pressures and roles and is no longer the nineteenth-century stereotype of the striped pants diplomat whispering code words to the allies. He presides over a complex establishment with responsibilities for defense, Peace Corps, cultural affairs, intelligence, information, agriculture, labor, and many other areas. His job is to coordinate, transact, motivate, and integrate. He must be able to produce environments where the most competent people can realize their talents, coordinate their efforts, remain committed to organizational goals, and integrate their efforts in a manner that no one of them working alone could surpass.

This new concept of leadership embraces four important competencies: (1) knowledge of large, complex human systems, (2) practical theories of guiding these systems, theories that encompass methods for the seeding, nurturing, and integrating individuals and groups, (3) interpersonal competence, particularly the sensitivity to understand the effects of one's own behavior on others and how one's own personality shapes one's particular leadership style and value system, and (4) a set of values and competencies that enables one to know when to confront and attack, if necessary, and when to support and provide the psychological safety so necessary for growth.

It is amusing and occasionally frustrating to note that the present view of leadership, which I have referred to as an agricultural model, is often construed as "passive" or "weak" or "soft" or more popularly "permissive" and dismissed with the same uneasy, patronizing shrug one usually reserves for women who succeed, however clumsily, in playing a man's game. What is particularly interesting is that the role of leadership described here is clearly more demanding and formidable than any other historical precedent, from king to pope. It may be that construing this new leadership role in such passive and insipid terms may betray some anxiety aroused by the eclipse of a Victorian, distant, stern, and strict father. That may be the only kind of authority we have experienced firsthand and know intimately. Yet, if this new man of power—other-directed and interpersonally competent—emerges, as he now seems to be doing, then not only new myths and archetypes will have to be created to substitute for the old, familial ones but new ways will have to be developed to dramatize the advent of new heroes.

6

The Temporary Society

Except for one egregious gaffe, the American experience we forecast back in 1968—"temporary systems, nonpermanent relationships, turbulence, uprootedness, unconnectedness, mobility, and above all, unexampled social change"—seems, if anything, pallid and understated. I was taken aback to find that I referred to my outlook as "queer and grotesque." Now it strikes me as rather commonplace. Phrases like "embracing ambiguity," "identifying with the adaptive process," and "increasing our ability to collaborate" now appear as stale truths and, worse, the platitudes and banalities of the 1990s.[1]

I was reminded of this as I listened to an interview on National Public Radio of an editor of a hip, new business magazine, "Fast-Company"—a "zine," as he called it, for knowledge workers of "the new economy." The editor wondered if he was a little too "sunshiny" about the wonders of the information age, a little too "upbeat" about the staccato-like demands of the workplace. He was having second thoughts about deifying this big, bright, globally wired world.

I wonder, too, if the Brave New World we wrote about, with all of its churning and transitions, adequately considered the psychological and economic dislocations and costs inherent in the temporary society. Joseph Schumpeter, the theoretical architect of modern capitalism, immortalized it with his famous metaphor, the "gale of creative destruction." Later on, he became melancholy about capitalism and its discontents.

I don't think either one of us is melancholy today or were callous back then, but I don't think we took into account the shadowy side of change, the realization that every significant transition is a threat to one's self-esteem. Nor did we reckon with, let alone understand, the problems of the "underclass" in coping with social and personal changes. Just about everything we wrote about was—had to be— refracted through the prism of our own experience. And that experience, while not shallow, was pretty much that of two middle-class, well-educated, thirty-something white males trying hard to make sense of where our society was going.

For example, we didn't take into account the growing disparity between the nation's rich and its poor. When this book was published the income gap between the very rich and the very poor was at its narrowest: 1 percent of the population controlled about 18 percent of private wealth; now, 1 percent of the population controls 40 percent of the wealth. An obscene offshoot of this is that the average CEO of a large company now earns two hundred times more than the average worker, up from a forty-fold difference in the 1970s. Nor did we fully take into account what the chronic state of change (and anxiety) would mean to the workforce, especially these days when nearly everyone (aside from Silicon Valley workers) worries about getting a pink slip. One of the paradoxes of our current prosperity is that with all of the affluence, the ordinary citizen feels less and less satisfied. According to the University of Chicago's National Opinion Research Center, job satisfaction, financial satisfaction, and overall happiness are lower now than the average for the past twenty years. On top of that, all those competencies we glorified such as "learning how to enter groups and leave them," or "learning what roles are satisfying and how to attain them," or "learning how to develop intense and deep human relationships quickly—and learn how to 'let go'" have become daily grist for Dilbert's cynical cartoons.

Now to the gaffe I mentioned. Actually, to paraphrase a French aphorism, it was worse than a crime, it was a blunder. I'm referring to the chilling phrase, "The profession of a wife in an era of change is to provide continuity, the portable roots." I paid dearly for that. Soon after the book was published, during my days as provost of

SUNY-Buffalo, several women's groups occupied my office demanding an explanation and a retraction. So this is a thirty-year old retraction and apology for that colossal misjudgment. Before this section becomes longer than the chapter itself, I should end by reminding our readers that John Cage's couplet, the last words in this chapter, still stands, ageless, it seems, no less daunting and worth repeating.

—◦◉◦—

The American experience we write about—of temporary systems, nonpermanent relationships, turbulence, uprootedness, unconnectedness, mobility, and above all, unexampled social change—may sound queer and grotesque. "Nowhere but in America!" one can say, with either disgust or relief. Whatever reaction one chooses, one cannot avoid a dead reckoning with this social disorder we forecast—if one chooses to live in a modern society. For a characteristic feature of all modern (that is, industrialized) societies is the extent to which it is possible for people to change occupational and social position. "We will all be Americans someday!" shouted the angry young man in John Osborne's *Look Back in Anger*. And to the extent that nations become modernized, they will all share the American experience of becoming a temporary society.

"Someday," of course, may be a long time off for a Mexican peasant or Turkish villager. Daniel Lerner's classical study of Turkish villagers illustrated poignantly the meaning of place, of home, of rootedness. When the traditional Turk was asked where he would live if he could not live in Turkey, he responded, "I would rather die than live. I would not want to go anywhere. If all go I would go. If nobody goes I would choose death."[2] But life changes more quickly than we think. A newspaper arrives, a telephone, television, movies, a road, then a bus to the city. Nothing could be more revolutionary than a road.

One advantage of life in a so-called developing society, beset by poverty and disease, is the ability to "see" the future, so to speak, before it happens; that is, an alternative future, as expressed in the great industrialized states. Seeing the future in the present is very like the science fiction of H. G. Wells's time-machine. And this is possible only by the queer conjunction of simultaneous existence of societies at markedly different stages of economic, political, and social development coupled with the mass media, which transmit these images to all nations at any scale of development, from primitive villages to urban complexes. The advantage I speak of is the potential to *seize* the future through the examination and evaluation of the social and moral consequences of change before they invade—like a night train that suddenly appears, out of nowhere.

Whereas it is too late to slow down the pace of temporary societies, it is not too late (and it becomes necessary) to examine ways that may be more adaptive in coping with temporary systems, ways that could both realize our full human potentialities and extract whatever benefits modernization can bring. What follows are some fragmentary and personal thoughts on this question, which each reader must ultimately resolve for himself.

First, we must eternally confront and test our humanness and strive to become more fully human. The psychological consequences of temporary relationships are discussed in Chapter Four. We operate on a narrow range of the full spectrum of human potential, and for the most part, our organizational lives tend to compress the possibilities even more. Organization, by definition and certainly in practice, implies differentiation of function and specialization. Groups and interpersonal relationships tend to reinforce, if not worsen, this narrowness by calling on fewer and more stable and predictable functions. Essentially this is what the games-people-play is all about, a highly ritualized and complex habit that draws predictable responses from others so that one can play with ease, certainty, and without development. That's what make these games boring, like bad theater. These games can, of course, be rewarding and exhilarating, but most of the time they constrict their players to narrower and narrower lives, often compulsive and imprisoning.

Fritz Redl once referred to these complicated social gambits as "role
uction," and in his pre-LSD days, Timothy Leary used the phrase
'interpersonal reflex" to denote the same phenomenon.

To be more fully human means that we must work hard at com-
ng to terms with unfamiliar aspects of our personalities, and it
neans we have to work equally hard to get other people to widen
heir responses so that they can understand and accept unfamiliar-
y and uncertainty. It also means that we must be able to perceive
ur *common* humanness without fear of absorption or nothingness.
The "obliteration of differences" that Slater mentions can produce
intense anxiety, particularly the fantasies associated with underlying human similarities.

"Working hard at it" means just that. As I have implied, there
are many forces conspiring against becoming fully human. Human
relations and organizational life are both predicated on the assumption of shared and stable expectations. I suspect that the recent
emergence on the American scene of such exciting and new educational ventures as Esalen, Western Behavioral Science Institute,
Kairos, and the National Training Laboratories reflects the intense
preoccupation with our humanness as well as the grim realization
that this very humanness is hard to preserve and project on the job.

Working hard at it also means that our society and particularly
our educational systems should be involved in helping to develop
the necessary interpersonal competencies rather than, as tends to
be true of most education, working against our full human development. Our educational system should (1) help us to identify with
the adaptive process without fear of losing our identity, (2) increase
our tolerance of ambiguity without fear of losing intellectual mas-
tery, (3) increase our ability to collaborate without fear of losing our
individuality, and (4) develop a willingness to participate in social
evolution while recognizing implacable forces. In short, we need an
educational system that can help us make a virtue out of contingency rather than one which induces hesitancy or its reckless com-
panion, expedience.

Most education shies away from or shuns these adaptive capacities, wishfully hoping that the student will possess them or that, like sex, he can find out about them from his buddies. So for the most part we learn the significant things informally and badly, having to unlearn them later on in life when the consequences are grave or frightfully expensive, like a five-day-a-week analysis.

I would like to see educational programs in the art and science of being more fully human, which would take very seriously the kind of world we are living in and help produce students who could not only cope with and understand this world but attempt to change it. We should help our students develop the necessary interpersonal competencies, which would include at least the following: (1) learning how to develop intense and deep human relationships quickly—and learn how to "let go." In other words, learning how to get love, to love, and to lose love; (2) learning how to enter groups and leave them; (3) learning what roles are satisfying and how to attain them; (4) learning how to widen the repertory of feelings and roles available; (5) learning how to cope more readily with ambiguity; (6) learning how to develop a strategic comprehensibility of a new "culture" or system and what distinguishes it from other cultures; and finally, (7) learning how to develop a sense of one's uniqueness.

One final consideration, which I suspect our educational system cannot provide, nor can we hope to acquire it easily: Somehow with all the mobility, chronic churning and unconnectedness we envisage, it will become more and more important to develop some permanent or abiding commitment. If our libidinal attachments, to return to a theme of Slater's, become more diffused, it will be essential that we focus commitment on a person or an institution or an idea. This means that as general commitments become diffuse or modified, a greater *fidelity* to something or someone will be necessary to make us more fully human.

For some, the commitment may be derived from marriage. I wrote in Chapter Three that "The profession of a wife in an era of change is to provide continuity, the portable roots." For others, a profession, work, the church, or some group may emerge as the source of fidelity. Ultimately, the world will require us to rely most heavily on our own resources. Hell, to paraphrase Sartre, may not be other people, but "the others" cannot always provide the sustenance and love that are so critical. We die alone and to a certain extent we must live alone, with a fidelity to ourselves. John Cage wrote a little "poem" that works as a proverb for our age and hopefully works as well as a tribute to the temporary society:

We carry our homes
within us
which enables us to *fly*.[3]

Notes

Preface to the Revised Edition

1. F. Capra. *The Web of Life*, New York: Anchor, 1996; J. Gleick, *Chaos: Making a New Science*, New York: Viking, 1987; P. Slater, *A Dream Deferred*, Boston: Beacon Press, 1991.

Chapter One

1. The original essay appeared in the March-April 1964 issue of the *Harvard Business Review*.

2. W. G. Bennis. *On Becoming a Leader*. New York: Addison-Wesley, 1989.

3. P. Slater. *A Dream Deferred*. Boston: Beacon Press, 1991.

4. J. Sniezek and R. Henry. "Accuracy and Confidence in Group Judgment." *Organizational Behavior and Human Decision Process Journal*, 1989, pp. 1–28

5. F. Capra. *The Web of Life*. New York: Anchor, 1996.

6. M. Rosenblum. "Growing Prosperity, Hope Changes the Face of Africa." Associated Press, Nov. 31, 1997.

7. R. T. Eisler. *The Chalice and the Blade*. New York: Harper & Row, 1987; *Sacred Pleasure*. San Francisco: Harper San Francisco, 1996.

8. M. Gimbutas. *The Goddesses and Gods of Old Europe*, Berkeley: University of California Press, 1974; J. Mellaart, *Catal Huyuk*, New York: McGraw-Hill, 1967; J. Mellaart, *The Neolithic of the Near East*,

New York: Scribners, 1975; N. Platon, *Crete*, Geneva: Nagel Publishers, 1996.

9. R. T. Eisler. *Sacred Pleasure*. San Francisco: Harper San Francisco, 1996.

10. P. Slater. *A Dream Deferred*. Boston: Beacon Press, 1991.

11. E. E. Lawler. *From the Ground Up*. San Francisco: Jossey-Bass, 1996.

12. W. Adams and J. W. Brock. *The Bigness Complex*. New York: Pantheon, 1986.

13. For a complete review of this work see W. G. Bennis, "Effecting Organizational Change: A New Role for the Behavioral Scientist," *Administrative Science Quarterly*, September, 1963; and C. Argyris, "T-Groups for Organizational Effectiveness," *Harvard Business Review*, March-April, 1964.

14. W. G. Bennis, "Toward a 'Truly' Scientific Management: The Concept of Organizational Health," *General Systems Yearbook*, 1962, p. 273.

15. It would be a mistake to ignore the fact that there are many tasks for which the military-bureaucratic model is best suited, but it is precisely these tasks which are most vulnerable to automation.

16. N. Sanford, "Social Science and Social Reform," Presidential Address for SPSSI, Washington, D.C., August 28, 1958.

17. J. R. Oppenheimer, "On Science and Culture," *Encounter*, October, 1962, p. 5.

18. J. R. Killian, Jr., "The Crisis in Research," *The Atlantic Monthly*, March, 1963, p. 71.

19. M. Gardner, *Relativity for the Million* (New York: Macmillan, 1962), p. 11.

20. For a fuller discussion of this trend, see T. Levitt, "Marketing Myopia," *Harvard Business Review*, July-August, 1960, p. 45.

21. M. McLuhan, *Understanding Media* (New York: McGraw-Hill, 1964), p. 251.

22. I. Edman (ed.), *The Philosophy of Santayana* (New York: Random House, 1936).

23. Cf. O. Handlin, *The Uprooted* (Boston: Little, Brown, 1951),
    pp. 252–253; and K. Geiger, "Changing Political Attitudes in
    Totalitarian Society: A Case Study of the Role of the Family,"
    World Politics, January, 1956, pp. 187–205.

Chapter Two

1. E. Goffman, *Asylums.* New York: Anchor Press, 1961.

2. W. G. Bennis, "Toward a 'Truly' Scientific Management: The Concept of Organizational Health," *General Systems Yearbook,* 1962,
   p. 273. Herbert Spencer implied the same thing in his discussion of
   the transition from "militant" to "industrial" society; see C. W. Mills
   (ed.), *Images of Man* (New York: Braziller, 1960), p. 319.

3. Service calls this the Law of the Local Discontinuity of Progress.
   See E. R. Service, "The Law of Evolutionary Potential," in
   M. D. Sahlins and E. R. Service, *Evolution and Culture* (Ann
   Arbor: University of Michigan Press, 1960), pp. 98 ff.

4. See E. E. Hagen, *On the Theory of Social Change* (Homewood, Ill.:
   Dorsey, 1962), esp. pp. 26–30. This shows the folly of our foreign
   aid program, which tends, as a result of the anti-communist obsession that governs it, to keep power and influence in the hands of
   those least likely to use it innovatively.

5. W. J. Goode, *World Revolution and Family Patterns* (New York: Free
   Press, 1963), p. 355.

6. N. B. Ryder, "The Cohort in the Study of Social Change," *American
   Sociological Review,* vol. 30, 1965, pp. 843–861. This is a temporal
   version of Service's law. For another analysis of the problem see
   K. Mannheim, "The Problem of Generations," in P. Kecskemeti
   (ed.), *Essays on the Sociology of Knowledge* (London: Routledge and
   Kegan Paul, 1952), pp. 276–320.

7. Many of these points were made by Kingsley Davis in his classic
   paper "The Sociology of Parent-Youth Conflict," in R. L. Coser
   (ed.), *The Family: Its Structure and Functions* (New York: St. Martin's, 1964), pp. 455–471.

8. Ryder, *American Sociological Review,* p. 852.

9. What follows is a piece of speculative reconstruction, sandwiched between slices of observation. As such it is probably vulnerable in detail, and certainly oversimplified.

10. M. Zborowski, and E. Herzog, *Life Is With People* (New York: Schocken, 1962). This insulation was an important factor in protecting the culture for centuries against dilution.

11. Zborowski and Herzog, *Life Is With People*, pp. 131–141, 223–224, 232. During the frequent pogroms, however, these protectors became persecutors against whom there was no protection.

12. Zborowski and Herzog, *Life Is With People*, pp. 330–334.

13. Zborowski and Herzog, *Life Is With People*, pp. 142–151, 271.

14. This should not be overdrawn, however. The learned patriarch was less dominant than he was supposed to be in the old system, while in the new one maternal dominance tends to be highly diluted (as in most cultures) by male occupational success.

15. M. Mead, *New Lives for Old* (New York: Mentor, 1961), p. 22.

16. M. Mead, *Growing Up in New Guinea* (New York: Mentor, 1953), pp. 14–16, 37–38, 55–61, 80–83, 99, 128–133.

17. Mead, *New Lives for Old*, pp. 145 ff.

18. Mead, *New Lives for Old*, pp. 39, 51, 95, 103, 196, 352–354.

19. Mead, *New Lives for Old*, pp. 374–377.

20. Goode, *World Revolution and Family Patterns*, pp. 6–7.

21. The same may be said for the factory system whose democratizing influence is argued by A. W. Calhoun. See *A Social History of the American Family* (Cleveland: Arthur H. Clark, 1917–1919), vol. II, p. 198.

22. F. J. Turner, *The Frontier in American History* (New York: Holt, 1921). See Calhoun, *A Social History of the American Family*, vol. II, p. 169.

23. G. W. Pierson, "The M-factor in American History," in M. McGiffert (ed.), *The Character of Americans* (Homewood, Ill.: Dorsey, 1964), pp. 120–121.

24. See F. F. Furstenberg, Jr., "Industrialization and the American Family: A Look Backward," *American Sociological Review*, vol. 31, 1966, pp. 326–337. Furstenberg shows convincingly that the democratic family antedates urbanization and industrialization.

25. A. de Tocqueville, *Democracy in America* (New York: Oxford University Press, 1947), p. 386.

26. Calhoun, *A Social History of the American Family*, vol. I, p. 76; vol. III, pp. 144, 169–170. Calhoun is more concerned with the growth of feminine "parasitism" and child neglect, which he sees as attendant upon the growth of a wealthy class in the East. *A Social History of the American Family*, vol. II, pp. 227 ff.; vol. III, pp. 131 ff.

27. See for example, Calhoun, *A Social History of the American Family*, vol. II, pp. 51–77; vol. III, pp. 131–156; S. M. Lipset, "A Changing American Character?" in McGiffert, *The Character of Americans*, pp. 302–330; and Furstenberg, *American Sociological Review*, pp. 326 ff.

28. See R. Sunley, "Early 19th Century American Literature on Child Rearing," in M. Mead and M. Wolfenstein (eds.), *Childhood in Contemporary Cultures* (Chicago: The University of Chicago Press, 1963), pp. 159–161.

29. Calhoun, *A Social History of the American Family*, vol. II, pp. 51–67.

30. Calhoun, *A Social History of the American Family*, vol. III, pp. 144–145, 166. See Goode, *World Revolution and Family Patterns*, pp. 6–7.

31. See M. Wolfenstein, "Fun Morality: An Analysis of Recent American Child-Training Literature," in Mead and Wolfenstein, *Childhood in Contemporary Cultures*, p. 169.

32. Calhoun, *A Social History of the American Family*, vol. III, pp. 131, 141–148.

33. Calhoun. See *A Social History of the American Family*, vol. II, pp. 66–67; vol. III, p. 152.

34. Calhoun. See *A Social History of the American Family*, vol. I, pp. 132–144; E. S. Morgan, *The Puritan Family* (New York: Harper & Row, 1966), pp. 33 ff., 62–64, 77–78, 124–130, 171.

35. Morgan, *The Puritan Family*, pp. 12, 18–19, 97–98. It has often been observed, however, that other Puritan beliefs served to inhibit this authoritarianism. See H. Israel, "Some Influence of Hebraic Culture on Modern Social Organization," *American Journal of Sociology*, vol. 71, 1966, pp. 384–394.

36. Morgan,*The Puritan Family*, pp. 20–21, 45–52, 65 ff., 77–78, 83–84, 87 ff., 106–108, 147–149. See Calhoun, *A Social History of the American Family*, vol. I, pp. 142–144.

37. Morgan, *The Puritan Family*, pp. 30, 71–75, 83–86, 103–108.

38. Morgan, *The Puritan Family*, pp. 160, 168–185.

39. P. Ariès, *Centuries of Childhood* (New York: Knopf, 1962).

40. Ariès, *Centuries of Childhood*, pp. 378, 411–413. The modern interest in childhood, education, and social change appeared also in ancient Greece and Rome. Ariès states that there were no portrayals of childhood life in the Middle Ages, but this was a popular theme for Greek and Roman artists. See V. Ehrenberg, *The People of Aristophanes* (Oxford: Blackwell, 1951), p. 197; and H. Blümner, *The Home Life of the Ancient Greeks* (New York: Funk and Wagnalls, n.d.), pp. 78 ff.

41. There is a strong positive correlation between respect for the aged, traditionalism, and authoritarianism cross culturally. See P. E. Slater, "Cultural Attitudes toward the Aged," *Geriatrics*, vol. 18, 1963, pp. 308–314. It receives its first historical expression in ancient comparisons between Athens and Sparta, the Athenians being criticized for lacking all three. See Xenophon, *Memorabilia*, III, 5, 13–16. See also Plato, *Republic*, 562E.

42. This paradox did not altogether escape Plato in his utopian musings. Like most utopian thinkers he wanted to isolate the children from noxious parental influence and bring them up according to his own plan. Whereas the Students for a Democratic Society slogan advocates mistrust of anyone over thirty, Plato wanted to eliminate everyone over ten (this is of course much too late for the kind of character molding he wanted, but Plato's psychology was at best primitive). The analogy is deliberate—a reminder that utopian

strivings, however conservative in intent, always drive a wedge between cohorts.

Plato then tries to counteract the powerful loosening force which this would set into motion by rigid and continuing controls over the socialization process, allowing no change or innovation even in children's play activities: see Plato, *Republic*, 540E; *Laws*, 797–798. This supports the hypothesis of one of my students, Harry Levine, that the democratization resulting from community usurpation of parental functions may spring from the fact that in practice such an arrangement leads to peer group socialization. For adult substitute-socializers can never approximate parents in number, almost by definition, and this gap is filled by the peer group. Plato seems to be expressing some dim awareness of this in his fear of children's games.

43. D. Mace and V. Mace, *The Soviet Family* (Garden City, N.Y.: Doubleday, 1964), p. 307. W. N. Stephens, in his book *The Family in Cross-Cultural Perspective* (New York: Holt, Rinehart and Winston, 1963), pp. 326–339, presents data showing the isomorphism between family and state authority patterns. He then argues that the direction of causality is from state to family, but provides no real basis for rejecting the idea of mutual causality.

44. L. A. Coser, "The Case of the Soviet Family," in Rose L. Coser (ed.), *The Family: Its Structure and Functions* (New York: St. Martin's Press, 1964), pp. 527–528, 540. In a personal communication Coser suggests that one of the most important factors tending toward democratization of the postwar German family was the ability of the young to adapt more successfully to the occupation—often making more money (in the black market or providing various services to Americans) than their skilled but discredited fathers.

45. Coser, *The Family*, p. 527.

46. Mace and Mace, *The Soviet Family*, p. 316.

47. Coser, *The Family*, p. 539.

48. Mace and Mace, *The Soviet Family*, p. 317; Coser, *The Family*, pp. 539–540.

49. Goode, *World Revolution and Family Patterns*, pp. 313–315.

50. M. E. Spiro, *Children of the Kibbutz* (New York: Schocken, 1965), pp. 357 ff., 367 ff.; and Yonina Talmon-Garber, "The Case of Israel," in Coser, *The Family*, pp. 613–617.

51. S. Diamond, "Collective Child-Rearing: The Kibbutz," in Coser, *The Family*, pp. 430–431; Spiro, *Children of the Kibbutz*, pp. 11 ff., 340, 384–388.

52. Coser, *The Family*, pp. 376–382.

53. K. Erikson, *Wayward Puritans* (New York: Wiley, 1966), p. 39.

54. Calhoun, *A Social History of the American Family*, vol. III, pp. 174–175.

Chapter Three

1. A. de Tocqueville, *Democracy in America*, J. P. Mayer and M. Lerner, eds. (New York: Harper & Row, 1966).

2. J. R. Oppenheimer, "Prospects in the Arts and Sciences," *Perspectives USA*, 1955, pp. 10–11.

3. Of course, size alone will not necessarily lead to the end of bureaucratic machinery—witness the federal government. But, even there, the mounting size and scope is leading to a neo-Jeffersonian approach with increasing responsibility sequestered by state and local agencies.

4. Let me propose a hypothesis to explain this tendency. It rests on the assumption that man has a basic need for transcendental experiences, somewhat like the psychological rewards that William James claimed religion provided—"an assurance of safety and a temper of peace, and, in relation to others, a preponderance of loving affections." Can it be that as religion has become secularized, less transcendental, men search for substitutes such as close interpersonal relationships, psychoanalysis—even the release provided by drugs such as LSD?

5. M. Beerbohm, *Zuleika Dobson* (London: Folio Society, 1966), p. 126.

6. C. Clark, "Oxford Reformed," *Encounter*, January, 1965, p. 48.

7. C. Kerr, *The Uses of the University* (Cambridge, Mass.: Harvard University Press, 1964), p. 86.

8. P. Drucker, *The Practice of Management* (New York: Harper & Row, 1954), p. 167.

9. R. R. Blake and J. S. Mouton, *The Managerial Grid* (Houston: Gulf Publishing, 1964).

10. J. Rabbie, verbal communication, 1966.

11. E. Erikson, "Ontogeny of Ritualization," paper presented to the Royal Society, June, 1965.

12. A. de Tocqueville, *Democracy in America*.

Chapter Four

1. The immediate stimulus for this chapter was a conversation with Paul Campanis in which some of these questions were discussed, and I would like to express my appreciation for whatever this chapter owes to that encounter.

2. The intimate connections between industrial and family patterns drawn in this book may puzzle some readers, for since the industrial revolution we are used to thinking of them as separate spheres. There are many indications, however, that they are once again converging, as we shall see. For another analysis of these interrelationships see E. Litwak, "Technological Innovation and Ideal Forms of Family Structure in an Industrial Democratic Society," unpublished manuscript, University of Michigan School of Social Work, Ann Arbor, 1966.

3. G. W. Pierson, "The M-factor in American History," in M. McGiffert (ed.), *The Character of Americans* (Homewood, Ill.: Dorsey, 1964), pp. 119 ff.

4. Today, however, a fully human individual would be experienced as unique, strange, inconsistent, contradictory.

5. The American preoccupation with deodorizing themselves and their environment leads, as Edward Hall points out, to the underdevelopment of olfaction and "a land of olfactory blandness and

sameness that would be difficult to duplicate anywhere else in the world." Since smell serves both to differentiate individuals and to identify their emotional state, this de-emphasis of olfaction con- tributes much to the achievement of interchangeability, although of a purely negative and superficial kind. Hall also observes that the suppression of olfactory sensation obscures memory "because smell evokes much deeper memories than either vision or sound." See E. T. Hall, *The Hidden Dimension* (Garden City, N.Y.: Doubleday, 1966), pp. 43–44. This serves the same function as does childhood schooling—quarantining the individual from the contagion of the past (see Chapter II).

6. See, for example, Hall, *The Hidden Dimension*, pp. 7–37; K. Lorenz, *On Aggression* (New York: Harcourt, Brace, 1966); and J. P. Scott, *Animal Behavior* (Chicago: The University of Chicago Press, 1958), pp. 206 ff.

7. M. R. Koller, "Residential and Occupational Propinquity," in R. F. Winch, R. McGinnis, and H. R. Barringer (eds.), *Selected Studies in Marriage and the Family* (New York: Holt, Rinehart, and Winston, 1962), pp. 472–477; L. Festinger, S. Schachter, and K. Back, *Social Pressures in Informal Groups* (New York: Harper, 1950); W. H. Whyte, Jr., *The Organization Man* (Garden City, N.Y.: Doubleday, 1956), pp. 365–386; M. Mead, "We Are All Third Gen- eration," in McGiffert, *The Character of Americans*, pp. 131–141.

8. As Simmel observed some time ago in his analysis of "social circles," see G. Simmel, *Conflict and the Web of Group-Affiliations* (New York: The Free Press, 1964), pp. 127 ff.

9. In a sense we are discussing the re-invention, at the human level, of "flocking." Lorenz points out that species characterized by flocking do not recognize individuals at all, and any permanence in specific relationships (such as mating) is entirely dependent upon stability in extrinsic situational factors. While it is doubtful that humans will ever lose altogether the ability to discriminate among individuals, the evolution of interchangeability can be viewed as a legitimate cultural analogue of flocking. Since Lorenz argues that the recog- nition of individuals is indissolubly linked with intraspecific ag- gression—a trait which has clearly become nonfunctional for

humans—its atrophy might be accompanied by some benefits. See Lorenz, *On Aggression*, p. 148.

10. A paper by Ruth Jacobs suggests that the popularity of sensitivity training groups, therapy groups, basic-encounter groups, and the like may be derived from the same impulse that founded the utopian communities of nineteenth-century America. Both express a desire for total community involvement, for fraternity, for self-development, for a haven from competitive and detached social relationships, and so on. Both share certain mechanisms, such as public confession, and a messianic faith in love, honesty, and trust as solutions to social problems. See R. Jacobs, "The Therapeutic Group as the New American Utopian Community," unpublished manuscript, Brandeis University. It should be emphasized, however, that these traits emerge spontaneously in groups of this kind regardless of, and often in spite of, the ideological predilections of the leaders.

11. D. Riesman, N. Glazer, and R. Denney, *The Lonely Crowd* (Garden City, N.Y.: Doubleday, 1955), pp. 37–38.

12. Riesman, Glazer, and Denney, *The Lonely Crowd*, pp. 31 ff.

13. M. Wolfenstein, "Fun Morality: An Analysis of Recent American Child-Training Literature," in M. Mead and M. Wolfenstein (eds.), *Childhood in Contemporary Cultures* (Chicago: The University of Chicago Press, 1963), pp. 168–178.

14. For a more thoughtful analysis of the impact of technology on family functions, see Litwak, "Technological Innovation and Ideal Forms of Family Structure," pp. 7–13.

15. E. Bott, *Family and Social Network* (London: Tavistock, 1957), p. 198; M. Komarovsky, *Blue-Collar Marriage* (New York: Random House, 1964); M. Young and P. Willmot, *Family and Kinship in East London* (Baltimore: Pelican, 1964); P. E. Slater, "Parental Role Differentiation," *American Journal of Sociology*, vol. 67, 1961, pp. 296–308; Litwak, *op cit.*, p. 14.

16. But see K. G. Hillman, "Marital Instability and Its Relation to Education, Income, and Occupation: An Analysis Based on Census Data," in Winch et al., *Selected Studies in Marriage and the Family*, pp. 603–608.

17. See P. E. Slater, *Microcosm: Structural, Psychological, and Religious Evolution in Groups* (New York: Wiley, 1966), where the assumption made here—that whenever a small group, community, or large-scale society holds a conversation *as a group,* it is always commenting, directly or indirectly, on the strains in its own social structure—is considerably elaborated.

18. Our feeling that mobility is less possible for a wife than for a husband is deeply rooted in cultural tradition. Murdock found that mobility, not strength, was the only principle which universally distinguished men's from women's tasks. Women have generally been barred from mobile pursuits (such as hunting) by the encumbrances of pregnancy and childbirth. Technology, however, has rendered even this generality somewhat obsolete. See G. P. Murdock, "Comparative Data on the Division of Labor by Sex," *Social Forces,* vol. 15, 1937, pp. 551–553.

19. W. H. Whyte, Jr., "The Wife Problem," in Winch et al., *op cit.,* pp. 118 ff.

20. It is also usually discussed as if it were only an issue for middle-class mothers (just as delinquency is sometimes discussed as if having a father on the golf course and a mother at her bridge club were problems for the slum child). This is, of course, the opposite of the truth, except with regard to the problem I am concerned with here.

21. By the same token we increasingly derive our sense of identity not from a pattern of simultaneous group affiliations, but from a pattern of participation in events: "the *now* generation," "you are there," "where it's happening." To participate in a unique historical sequence becomes a desirable end. We are becoming cohort-oriented, each cohort with its pop favorites, events, and memory-trinkets. Ultimately, however, our disconnectedness is both spatial *and* temporal. This is somewhat disorienting, and gives rise to the modern obsession with concepts such as "self" and "identity." In our provincial manner we imagine these symptoms of contemporary social pathology to be universal human needs. But to require a consistent self-concept is itself a disease.

22. L. A. Coser, "Greedy Organizations," unpublished manuscript, Brandeis University, 1967.

23. See P. E. Slater, "Prolegomena to a Psychoanalytic Theory of Aging and Death," in R. Kastenbaum (ed.), *New Thoughts on Old Age* (New York: Springer, 1964), pp. 20 ff.

24. See G. Caplan, *Mental Health Aspects of Social Work in Public Health* (Berkeley: University of California School of Social Welfare, 1955), pp. 123 ff; L. J. Yarrow, "Separation from Parents During Early Childhood," in M. L. Hoffman and L. W. Hoffman (eds.), *Review of Child Development Research* (New York: Russell Sage Foundation, 1964), pp. 89–136.

25. See R. V. Burton and J.W.M. Whiting, "The Absent Father and Cross-Sex Identity," *Merrill-Palmer Quarterly*, vol. 7, 1961, pp. 85–95.

26. It seems safe to say that T-groups, basic-encounter groups, and the like will increase in popularity in any case, since they serve both to prepare for the fluid future we have envisioned, and to express these counterdrives.

Chapter Five

1. *Fortune*, December 29, 1997, p. 279.

2. Alexis de Tocqueville, "The Character of Americans," in *Democracy in America*, ed. by M. McGiffert, Dorsey Press, Homewood, Ill., pp. 61, 62.

3. V. R. Fuchs, "The First Service Economy," *The Public Interest*, #2, Winter 1966, p. 7.

4. At its National Congress, held in New York City on December 8, 1966, I exhorted the National Association of Manufacturers to change its name to the National Association of Management on this basis. The leading stories in that morning's *New York Times* dealt with the management or mismanagement of the Vietnam war, cities, hospitals, and universities.

5. C. Argyris, "Some Causes of Organizational Ineffectiveness Within the Department of State," *Occasional Papers*, no. 2, U.S. Department of State, 1967.

6. I am not recommending that organizations become like universities. To some extent they already are, that is, to the extent they are employing expensive professional talent. But university social

systems are poor models to emulate, partly because of a misplaced ethic of individualism and partly because of its correlate, no sense of community or supraindividual goals.

7. S. Freud, "On Narcissism," *Collected Papers* ((London: Hogarth Press, 1948), Vol. IV, p. 30.

8. A. M. Schlesinger, *The Coming of the New Deal* (Boston: Houghton Mifflin, 1959), p. 528.

9. E. Morison, *Man, Machines and Modern Times* (Cambridge, Mass.: M.I.T. Press, 1966), chap. 2.

10. Morison, *Man, Machines and Modern Times.*

11. E. Hamilton, *The Echo of Greece* (New York: W. W. Norton, 1957), p. 30.

12. S. Grinnell, "Organizational Development in a University." (Mimeo can be obtained by writing the author at Case Institute of Technology, Cleveland, Ohio.)

13. Specialism, by definition, implies a peculiar slant, a skewed vision of reality. McLuhan tells a good joke on this subject. A tailor went to Rome and managed to get an audience with His Holiness. Upon his return a friend asked him, "What did the Pope look like?" The tailor answered, "A 41 Regular."

14. In Sir George Thomson's book, *The Foreseeable Future,* he demonstrates the extraordinary power of the new biology to affect genic organization. When asked about its obvious applications for controlling the genic structure, he replied: "We might as well try to talk of improving a statue by spraying it with machine gun bullets." This reply might be interpreted as revealing not only a disbelief in applied science but also through its imagery, a certain hostility to it. (See G. Murphy, "Toward a Science of Individuality," in *Unfinished Tasks in the Behavioral Sciences* [Baltimore: The William and Wilkins Co, 1964] p. 202.)

15. C. Barnard, *The Functions of the Executive* (Cambridge, Mass.: Harvard University Press, 1938), p. 278.

16. I am referring to organizations such as TRW Systems, Union Carbide, American Airlines, Federated Department Stores, Polaroid, ALCAN, Hardwood-Weldon Mfg. Co., Hotel Corporation of America, and many others. See W. G. Bennis, *Changing Organizations* (New York: McGraw-Hill, 1966).

17. An example of this personification shows up daily in our foreign crises. Simply by replacing leaders (like Diem or Kanh or Ky, etc.) we delude ourselves that problems will be solved. Our problems with France, located in a complicated social matrix, will not end with the death of De Gaulle. De Gaulle doesn't exist in an environmental void; he embodies important policy differences between the United States and France.

18. D. Riesman, N. Glazer, and R. Denney, *The Lonely Crowd* (Garden City, N.Y.: Doubleday, 1955).

19. E. E. Lawler and L. W. Porter, "Antecedent Attitudes of Effective Managerial Performances," *Organizational Behavior and Human Performance*, vol. 2, pp. 122–142.

20. I am *not* arguing for conformity or gray, bland organization men. In fact, the opposite is true. Before individuals can be fully human and "self-actualized," organizational systems have to be developed that can cultivate the growth of *fully human* persons. We can never, in T. S. Eliot's words, "design systems so perfectly that no man needs be good."

21. R. Ash, *Fortune*, March, 1967, p. 153.

22. R. Bendix, *Max Weber: An Intellectual Portrait* (Garden City, N.Y.: Doubleday, 1960).

23. D. C. Pelz, "Freedom in Research," *International Science and Technology*, vol. 26, 1964, pp. 54–66.

Chapter Six

1. To take one recent example, an article in the *Los Angeles Times* (Jan. 18, 1998) on the movie business quoted David Friedman of M.I.T. as saying, "Think of each of these productions as a business that can run to $100 million. It just pops up like a mushroom, forms together, hires gazillions of contractors and, in three to six months, vanishes forever. It is the most flexible and remarkable business. And it happens over and over again."

2. D. Lerner, *The Passing of Traditional Society* (New York: The Free Press of Glencoe, 1958), p. 148.

3. J. Cage, *Silence* (Cambridge, Mass.: M.I.T. Press, 1966), p. 175.

Index

A

Academicians: competition among, 122; conflicting teaching versus research goals of, 82–83; isolation of, 119; managers collaboration with, 69–73; professional couples as, 103–104; stances of, 70–71. *See also* Universities

Action-research model: for leadership, 127–128; for organizational revitalization, 125–126

Acton, Lord, 23

Adams, W., 6

Adaptability: changing conditions and, 75, 78–79; as determinant of organizational survival, 2–3, 10, 11; leadership for, 120–122; as organizational problem, 75, 78–79; and trend towards the "organization man," 17

Adaptive organizations: adaptation of, 120–122; collaboration in, 118–120; identity of, 122–125; integration of organizational and individual goals in, 115–117; intellectual capital of, 111; leadership patterns for, 63–64, 83, 109–134; other-directedness in, 130; power distribution in, 117–118; revitalization in, 125–126; social territory

in, 127; system intervention in, 128–129; temporary systems in, 83–84, 105, 112–114. *See also* Business organizations

Adaptive structures, 83

Adaptive systems, 62–63. *See also* Temporary systems

Adult education, 117

Aesopianism, 129

Affluent Society, The, 71

Africa, 5

Age segregation, 37–40, 48–49, 50

Agricultural model of leadership, 131–134

Alienation: of leaders, 129; temporary systems and, 93–94

Ambassador role, 133–134

American family. *See* Democratic family

American Psychological Association, 124

Anderson, H. C., 27

Anomie, temporary systems and, 93–94

Apathy, 26

Argyris, C., 9

Ariès, P., 48, 50

Arnold, M., 71

Ash, R., 131

Asia, 5